HOW TO
DESIGN GRIDS
AND USE THEM EFFECTIVELY

ALAN SWANN

	1		2		3		4		5
1										
2										
3										
4										
5										
6										
7										
8										
9										
10										
11										
12										
13										
14										
15										
16										
17										
18										
19										
20										
21										
22										
23										
24										
25										
26										
27										
28										
29										
30										
31										
32										
33										
34										
35										
36										
37										
38										
39										

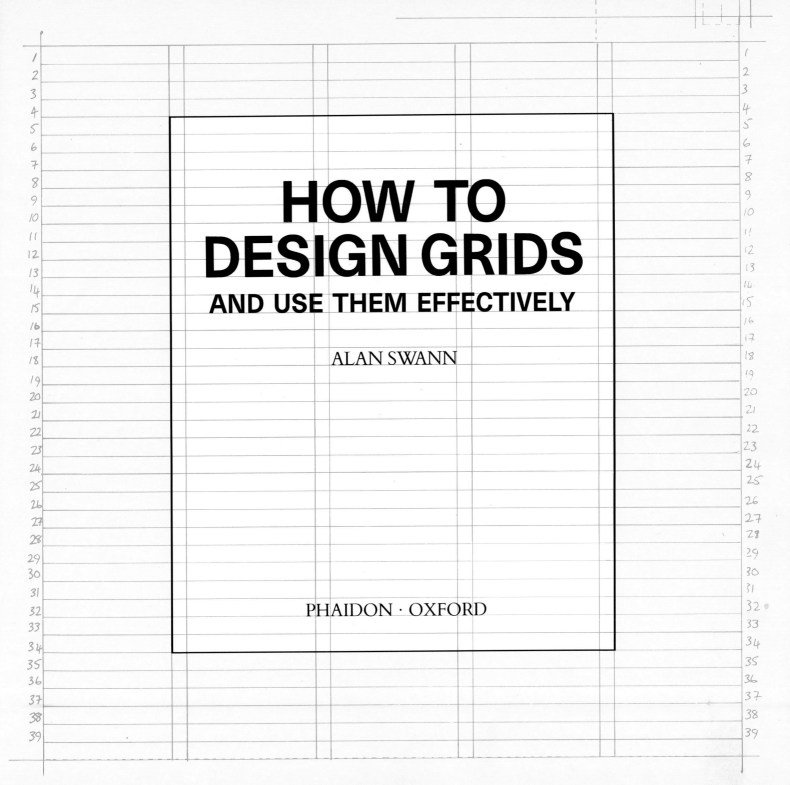

HOW TO
DESIGN GRIDS

AND USE THEM EFFECTIVELY

ALAN SWANN

PHAIDON · OXFORD

A QUARTO BOOK

Published by Phaidon Press Limited
Musterlin House
Jordan Hill Road
Oxford OX2 8DP

First published 1989
Copyright © 1989 Quarto Publishing plc

A CIP catalogue record for this book is available
from the British Library

ISBN 0 7148 2599 9

This book was designed and produced by
Quarto Publishing plc
The Old Brewery, 6 Blundell Street
London N7 9BH

Senior Editor Kate Kirby
Editor Lydia Darbyshire

Design Alan Swann
Artist David Kemp
Picture Research Sandra Bissoon

Art Director Moira Clinch
Editorial Director Carolyn King

Typeset by Ampersand, Bournemouth
Manufactured in Hong Kong by
Regent Publishing Services Ltd
Printed in Hong Kong

Special thanks to David Quay, Colin Theobald,
Croydon College Faculty of Art & Design
and Paul Diner

CONTENTS

INTRODUCTION

ONE OF THE GREAT MYSTERIES associated with any design process is simply how to start. When I began my career in graphic design the greatest problem I faced was how to arrange the design elements within a given space. This problem, which is familiar to both designers and artists, has led to the creation of certain rules and formulae. Artists have traditionally used compositional divisions that were created as far back as the earliest years of western civilization. The Roman architect Vitruvius devised a system of dividing an area mathematically which has been used to give visual balance to the subject matter of many paintings. Vitruvius' compositional ideas underpin some of the best known masterpieces of the past.

Similarly, the graphic design work that we see around us every day has been composed using guidelines and rules to order the information that is displayed in a balanced but creative manner.

The need for balance, structure and unity governs any form of visual imagery. In graphic design these qualities are often achieved through the careful control of measured space. Whenever you look at a piece of well-produced print, you should be able to detect quite clearly the formulae for precise measurements that underpin its creation. Space, in terms of the area of a design, can often be controlled and used dynamically when the number of design elements is limited. I am sure you have all seen brochures, posters and so on that carry a single word and perhaps a photograph or illustration, but the space around these elements absorbs you in the design. This rarely happens, however, and you will generally have to allow for lengthy text, headings, sub-headings, photographs, illustrations and all manner of supporting devices. To arrange these in an effective and powerful way that will influence the public, needs a formal approach to the arrangement of this jig-saw puzzle of elements.

How do you blend the linear formality of type with the flow of photography or illustration? How do you adjust the size, shape and visual balance of several elements to give the necessary emphasis to these elements in different ways? How can you use the space available to create an illusion of different depths of focus to the elements that are displayed?

The solution to these problems is to be found in the use of the grid. It is my belief that once you have fully grasped the compositional opportunities that grids can offer, you will be able to exploit to the full your ability to divide up a given area in mathematical terms. A grid is the geometric division of a space into precisely measured columns, spaces and margins. The columns represent the areas in which the body text will be aligned. The same divisions will be used to influence the position of other elements, such as large display type, and photographic and illustrative matter. In its simplest form the grid will help you to achieve the balanced appearance of a given space, even though this could appear dull and lifeless. If used unimaginatively a more dynamic and creative arrangement of the design elements will emerge when the grid is used with greater freedom. The grid may be compared with the stave used in a music score. The lines of the stave on the page represent a formal structure, but within this structure there is almost infinite freedom of expression. In much the same way, the structure of the lines representing the grid is merely the basis for your creative expression. The grid formation can also of course be used as a styling device in a family of design commissions or in the construction of on-going displays such as those used within a regularly published magazine, newspaper or journal. These are the more typical and obvious areas for which grids have been designed to give individuality to the publication's appearance. Once this styling has been established, the publication's character becomes unmistakable.

This book sets out to demonstrate the principles of the arrangement of elements within a grid format. It then explores the flexibility of the grid designs themselves. The later stages of the book show how a number of design projects have consciously and subconsciously been generated with the aid of a grid. The final section of the book shows, in some detail, how grids are used in the production process of design and describes the technical make-up of the grid itself.

Grids can often be taken for granted, but I am convinced that your design work will develop to a higher level if you first appreciate the value of planning with a grid. Regular, conscious practice with elements placed within a grid will develop your ability to manipulate composition and to generate good graphic design layouts.

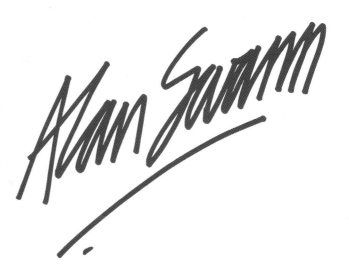

WHY GRIDS?

TO UNDERSTAND HOW GRIDS have evolved and to appreciate their purpose you must look back to the days when printing was in its infancy. Before the pioneer of printing, Gutenberg, introduced movable type, manuscripts were lovingly and painstakingly produced. Yet even in those early days, the conscious awareness of layout and design was clear for all to see. These works of art were rendered on a carefully proportioned grid: each letter form was drawn to a particular standard size, and the margins around the text were uniformly proportioned. To break up the visual monotony of rendered letter forms of regular size, some interesting design devices were applied. Some of the letter forms were enlarged to break in to the margin and create an illustrative shape for the text to run around. Occasionally, red was applied to the letters. This had two purposes: first, it was a design device that enhanced the script visually; second, it acted as a signal denoting a sentence, word or name of particular importance. Indeed, our language has been enriched by the use of red letters to denote Saints' or holy days, which in time have become known as "red letter days". Another device was the application of precious metals, such as gold, to the illustrated letter forms. These letters, which gave the illusion of brilliance when reflecting a light source, became known as "illuminated" letters.

The practices of the early monastic masters were superseded by mechanical printing processes. The best of the printers became masters themselves as they sought to manifest the best qualities of the past in their work. They followed the compositional layouts of the early manuscripts by setting their blocks of type in regular rows of equal length, spaced in ways that echoed the past. Unlike the work of the monastic scribes, however, the printers' type was cut as individual characters out of blocks of wood and set in rows to form words. These rows were held in clamp-like instruments known as sticks, and the lines of text themselves were set in a larger frame, creating equal columns of type. This process of typesetting was used up to recent times, although the wooden letters had been replaced by various forms of metal type.

To enable the printer to set his type in a print area,

structures and measuring devices were created. These devices could be transferred to a page in the form of guide lines, so creating a simple but accurate method of calculating the area for type, and later for illustrative components as well. In short, in the new mechanical age of mass production, grids evolved out of necessity.

Since type has now developed through the age of technology, these rigid, restrictive grids have become obsolete. However, the flexibility of type size and the ease with which it can be manipulated have given the designer more creative possibilities in composing the design space with a grid, which has now become the essential tool of the practising designer. By loosely drawing different grid shapes and sizes the designer can dictate his requirements to all those involved in the technical artwork process, and he has taken over this role from the master printers of the past. Traditionally, the printer controlled the reproduction of the visual image. Now the designer is in control.

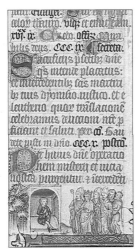

This hand-written manuscript, which dates from the Middle Ages, is structured on a carefully measured framework. The individual irregularities make the work quite unique.

This early text, printed by Caxton, was created using blocks of hand-carved wooden type set in a solid framework. Each printed sheet was lovingly prepared, making them works of art in their own right.

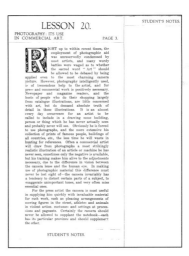

Early 20th-century metal type, set within a grid structure, was made up by hand from individual metal blocks of type and lines for rules; nevertheless it offers the capacity for mass-production.

Discovering grids

UNDERLYING THE VISUAL MATTER on nearly every piece of print – from the packaging and labelling of products to the daily newspapers with which we are all familiar – there is a formula or structure to be found. To discover how the designer has approached the task of arranging the elements in the design, you need to establish for yourself the designer's starting point for the piece of work.

This process is simple when you study a design with an abundance of text, as it is likely to be arranged within a fairly obvious grid structure. Most designs will have key margins around the elements, which will, although this is not always made obvious, be aligned to create a geometric unity. However, headings in larger type sizes, photographs, illustrations and all manner of graphic devices may be included in the layout, and these may not conform to the obvious pattern that the overall framework of the design has created.

To illustrate this point, I have taken some popular designs and have superimposed the grid structures underlying these designs.

These pieces of work range from simple, formal typographic structures to more complex, freer interpretations. In all the examples, however, you will see that their appearance has not been achieved by accident. The first stage of any piece of design work is the creation of a grid to guide the composition of the elements. This is the starting point that is common to all the areas of design that are explored in this book.

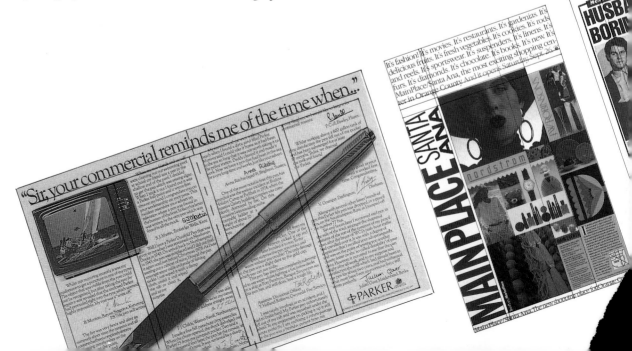

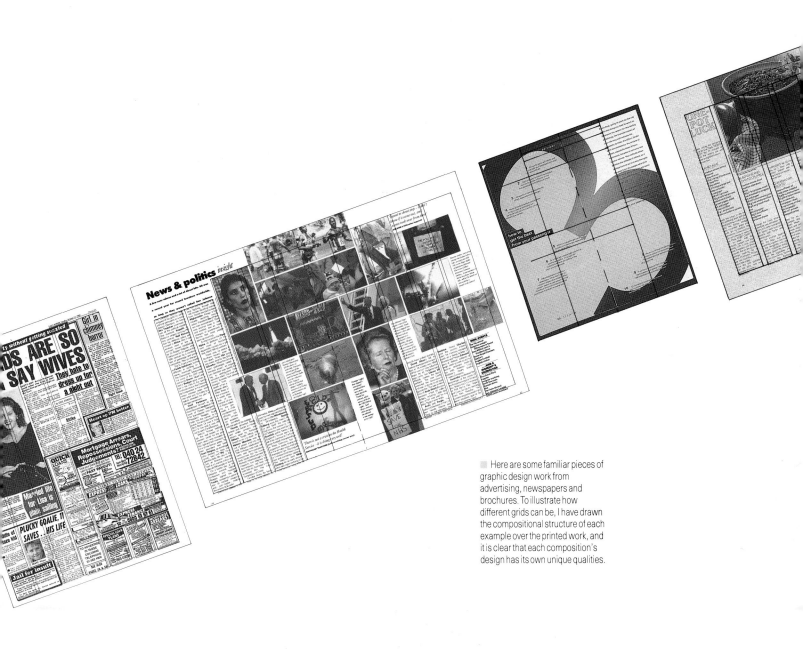

Here are some familiar pieces of graphic design work from advertising, newspapers and brochures. To illustrate how different grids can be, I have drawn the compositional structure of each example over the printed work, and it is clear that each composition's design has its own unique qualities.

Building a simple one-column grid

TO BEGIN WITH you must consider the structure and divisions of the design space available to you. The first and the simplest way to divide any space is to place a margin around the edge of the design area, creating a central zone for the design elements that are to appear. This margin can be drawn to any width or length, either to increase or decrease the display area within which you will work. Doing this automatically implies a sense of design in the work that will emerge. It would be beneficial, from this point on, for you to consider the grid design as providing the compositional structure of the work in hand. This initial discipline, although it seems restrictive, will, once you have mastered its use, actually give you great freedom.

On these pages you can see that an area can be divided to give different emphasis to the overall space. For instance, in the simple single-column design, the information would appear within the tinted area. (I have added this tint solely to underline the point I am making.) The single-column grid is, of course, the simplest of the options available to you. I refer to the area as a "column" because this space for the arrangement of type information on lines, one above the other, is similar in appearance and proportion to the great columns of public buildings in ancient Greece and Rome on which public information was displayed.

You can see from the examples on these pages that there are many formulae for dividing up the space that will be appropriate for the project in hand.

1

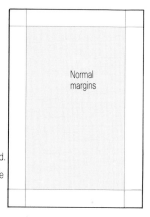

2

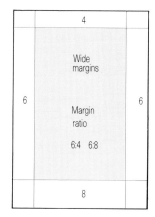

1 The simplest and easiest format has equal margins all round.

2 This luxurious formula, with wide margins on both sides, gives prominence and dignity to the printed matter.

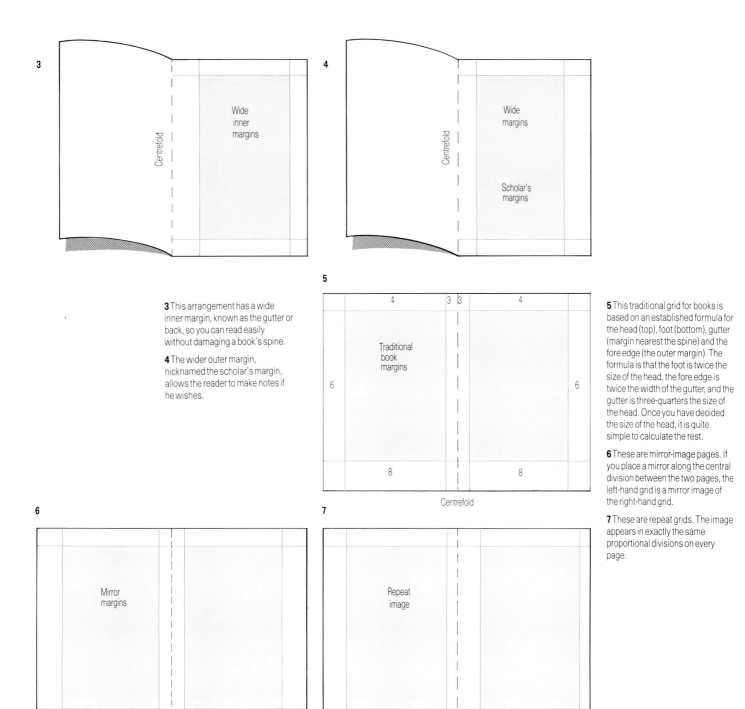

3 Wide inner margins

4 Wide margins / Scholar's margins

Centrefold

5 Traditional book margins

Centrefold

6 Mirror margins

Centrefold

7 Repeat image

Centrefold

3 This arrangement has a wide inner margin, known as the gutter or back, so you can read easily without damaging a book's spine.

4 The wider outer margin, nicknamed the scholar's margin, allows the reader to make notes if he wishes.

5 This traditional grid for books is based on an established formula for the head (top), foot (bottom), gutter (margin nearest the spine) and the fore edge (the outer margin). The formula is that the foot is twice the size of the head, the fore edge is twice the width of the gutter, and the gutter is three-quarters the size of the head. Once you have decided the size of the head, it is quite simple to calculate the rest.

6 These are mirror-image pages. If you place a mirror along the central division between the two pages, the left-hand grid is a mirror image of the right-hand grid.

7 These are repeat grids. The image appears in exactly the same proportional divisions on every page.

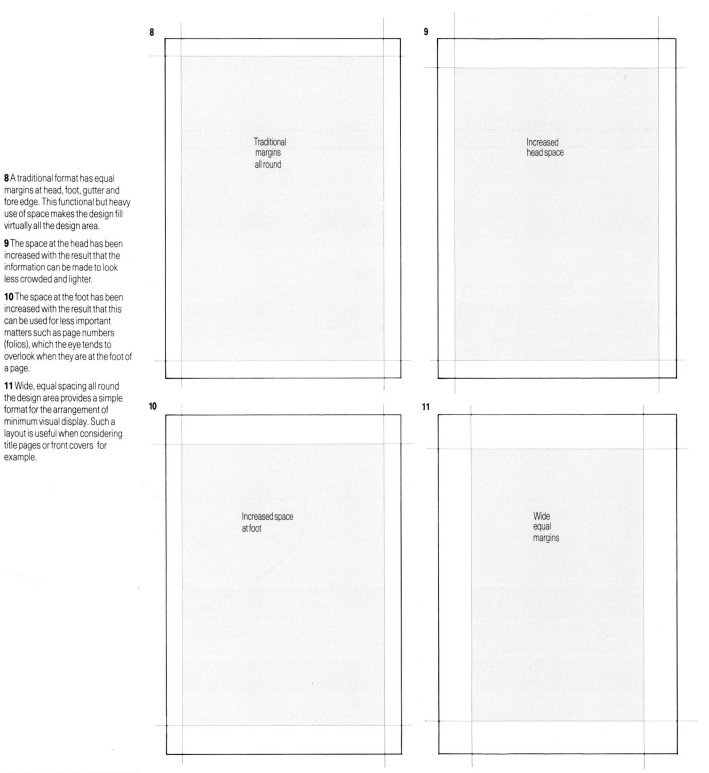

8 A traditional format has equal margins at head, foot, gutter and fore edge. This functional but heavy use of space makes the design fill virtually all the design area.

9 The space at the head has been increased with the result that the information can be made to look less crowded and lighter.

10 The space at the foot has been increased with the result that this can be used for less important matters such as page numbers (folios), which the eye tends to overlook when they are at the foot of a page.

11 Wide, equal spacing all round the design area provides a simple format for the arrangement of minimum visual display. Such a layout is useful when considering title pages or front covers for example.

8

Traditional
margins
all round

9

Increased
head space

10

Increased space
at foot

11

Wide
equal
margins

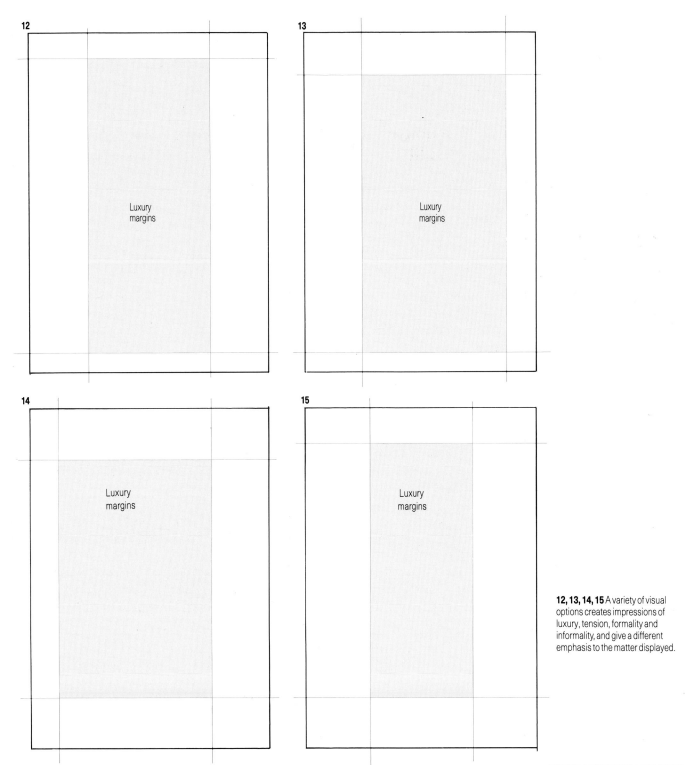

12

Luxury
margins

13

Luxury
margins

14

Luxury
margins

15

Luxury
margins

12, 13, 14, 15 A variety of visual options creates impressions of luxury, tension, formality and informality, and give a different emphasis to the matter displayed.

Paper sizes and shapes

BEFORE ANY GRID SHAPES and formulae can be devised, some consideration must be given to the paper or print surface on which the design is to appear. The economic use of paper, especially in long print runs, is essential, and it is your responsibility as a designer to bear this in mind. Your client will not wish to pay for paper that is simply thrown away. There are both metric and imperial paper sizes, and it will be necessary for you to enquire into the ranges your printer can accommodate. There are ways of dividing standard paper sizes into the shape that you wish to work on.

Regular sizes are used by the printer in the production of everyday print, and the European size most often used for brochures and leaflets is A4; the imperial equivalent would be foolscap. There are similar size equivalents in both ranges of paper sizes.

Taking the paper size as your base, fold or cut it into a shape that will give a distinctive quality to the design you are creating.

Once you have decided on a paper size and shape, you can begin to think about the process of developing a compatible grid composition or layout. Experiment with a number of grid options within the chosen shape to determine the suitability of the composition for the design concept.

To simplify this decision-making process, you may find it helpful to draw a number of grid formats on tracing paper and offer these up over the design areas. In this way, you will be able to respond quickly to the space and shape you are working on.

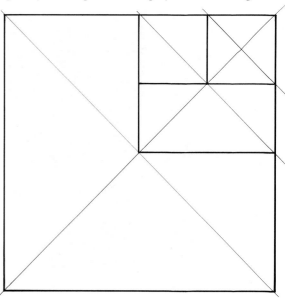

■ Choosing a paper size that is a division of the largest available size is economic and cost-effective. Locate the diagonals to determine quarters and plan further subdivisions. Your printer will give you the dimensions of the largest format, and once you have worked out approximate economic divisions, you can derive shapes from these proportions.

CHECKLIST

■ Establish the size of paper stock from which your design will be produced. This can be done as a simple thumbnail sketch.

■ Ensure that the cut or shape will be within the client's budget.

■ Draw the chosen shape.

■ Draw a number of grids on tracing paper.

■ Offer these up to the shape to see which is the most effective.

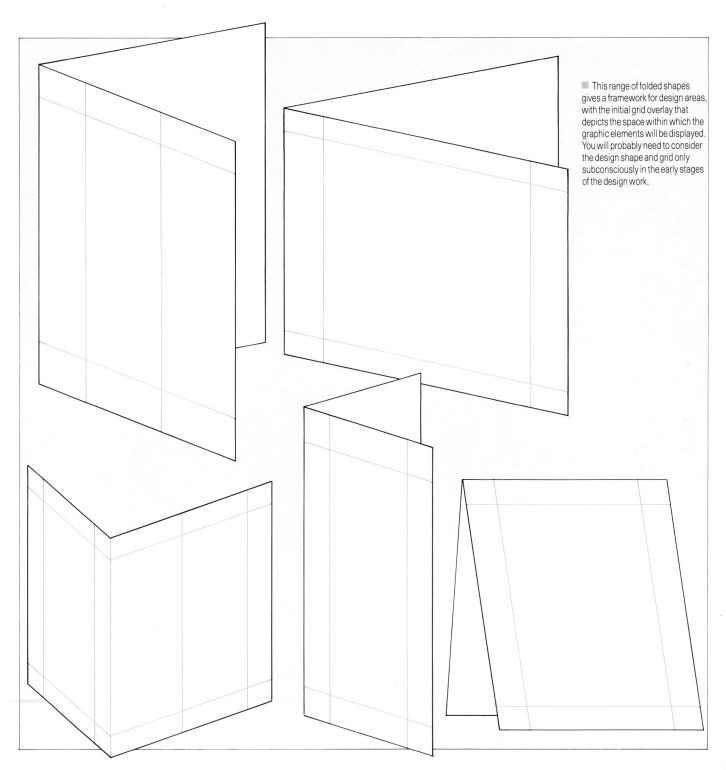

This range of folded shapes gives a framework for design areas, with the initial grid overlay that depicts the space within which the graphic elements will be displayed. You will probably need to consider the design shape and grid only subconsciously in the early stages of the design work.

Placing a heading on a simple grid

CHECKLIST

- Draw a number of different sized, single-column grids as thumbnail sketches.
- Produce these in light blue pencil or pen.
- Indicate different sized slabs of black using a heavy black marker or pieces of cut-out black paper.
- Vary the size of the heading slabs to give a different visual sensation.
- Notice how the composition of the grid changes the visual layout.

HAVING DRAWN A RANGE of single-column grid formations, you will be able to see how the design elements relate to this structure. At this point, I think it would be useful if you began to use a light blue pen or blue pencil to draw your grid layouts. I stress this method because in the later stages of the design process, when a grid underlies the design components that have been prepared for finished artwork, it will all be photographed and transferred to printing plates. Naturally, you will not wish to include the grid lines in the final print. Blue is used to define the grid because it is not picked up by the printer's camera. This does not mean that it is not possible to print blue, of course, as a special film is used for this purpose. Remember, most artwork is photographed as black and white and transformed into colour by the ink used in the printing press.

By indicating a heading within the grid and experimenting with its position and visual proportions, you will begin to establish the ways in which you can control the impact that the heading will have. You can also begin to see how the composition of the grid formulates an image within the design space.

Single column heading X

The heading can be indicated by drawing between two parallel lines. These parallel lines represent the "x" height, which denotes the body height of the lower case letters. Capital letters and the ascenders and descenders of the letter forms feature above and below these lines.

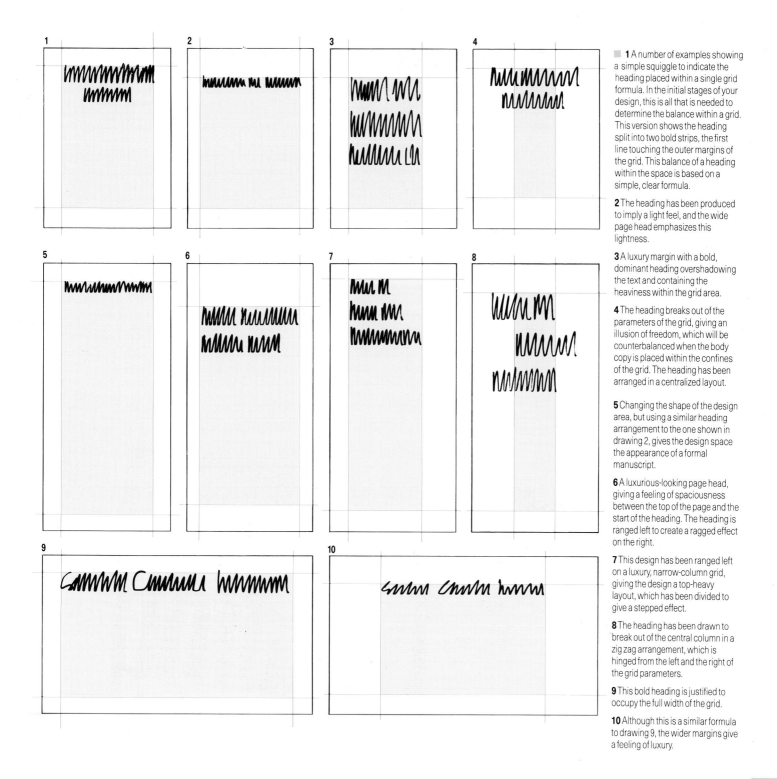

■ **1** A number of examples showing a simple squiggle to indicate the heading placed within a single grid formula. In the initial stages of your design, this is all that is needed to determine the balance within a grid. This version shows the heading split into two bold strips, the first line touching the outer margins of the grid. This balance of a heading within the space is based on a simple, clear formula.

2 The heading has been produced to imply a light feel, and the wide page head emphasizes this lightness.

3 A luxury margin with a bold, dominant heading overshadowing the text and containing the heaviness within the grid area.

4 The heading breaks out of the parameters of the grid, giving an illusion of freedom, which will be counterbalanced when the body copy is placed within the confines of the grid. The heading has been arranged in a centralized layout.

5 Changing the shape of the design area, but using a similar heading arrangement to the one shown in drawing 2, gives the design space the appearance of a formal manuscript.

6 A luxurious-looking page head, giving a feeling of spaciousness between the top of the page and the start of the heading. The heading is ranged left to create a ragged effect on the right.

7 This design has been ranged left on a luxury, narrow-column grid, giving the design a top-heavy layout, which has been divided to give a stepped effect.

8 The heading has been drawn to break out of the central column in a zig zag arrangement, which is hinged from the left and the right of the grid parameters.

9 This bold heading is justified to occupy the full width of the grid.

10 Although this is a similar formula to drawing 9, the wider margins give a feeling of luxury.

Headings and body copy

THE DESIGN ELEMENT that logically follows a heading is the text. Known as body copy, this will possibly be the most conventional element in the design. Body copy will use the grid to create a uniformity of composition by the way it is positioned. It will not normally break out of the blue guidelines but will be arranged in various typefaces, sizes, weights and shapes within this framework. It will be up to you to create interesting and relevant patterns with the body copy to enhance and give meaning to the design you are creating. The size of type, which is measured in the traditional point sizes or, more often these days, described in millimetres by measuring the X-height, will be controlled by the number of words required for the design. In these early visuals you need only achieve a happy visual balance between the position, shape and weight of heading and the pattern and feeling you describe in the body copy. It is important that you experiment with these elements to understand their visual differences.

1 A printed example of body text. This single example, which gives the impression of typesetting, is available in various point sizes, which will depend on the styling and copy specifications for your design.

2 Body type can be indicated as organized squiggles. If you draw in the "x" heights of the letters in pencil, it is simple to indicate in pen a uniform series of linking Ns (known as "N-ing") to give the impression of type. Sizes of type and the spacing can be selected in accordance with the job specifications.

3 Parallel straight lines can also be used to give the impression of body type. The lines can be produced in different weights of black and grey to characterize the body type weight and effect you want to achieve.

1 Culi fugitant uitantque tueri; sol etiam caecc tendere pergas propterea quia uis magnast ip aera per purum grauiter simulacra feruntur oculos turbantia composituras. Praeterea sp cumque est acer adurit saepe oculos, ideo qu possidet ignis multa, dolorem oculis quae gigr ando. Lurida praeterea fiunt quaecumque tue Aquati, quia luroris de corpore eorum ser fluunt simulacris. Culi fugitant uitantque tueri caecat, contra si tendere pergas propterea qu

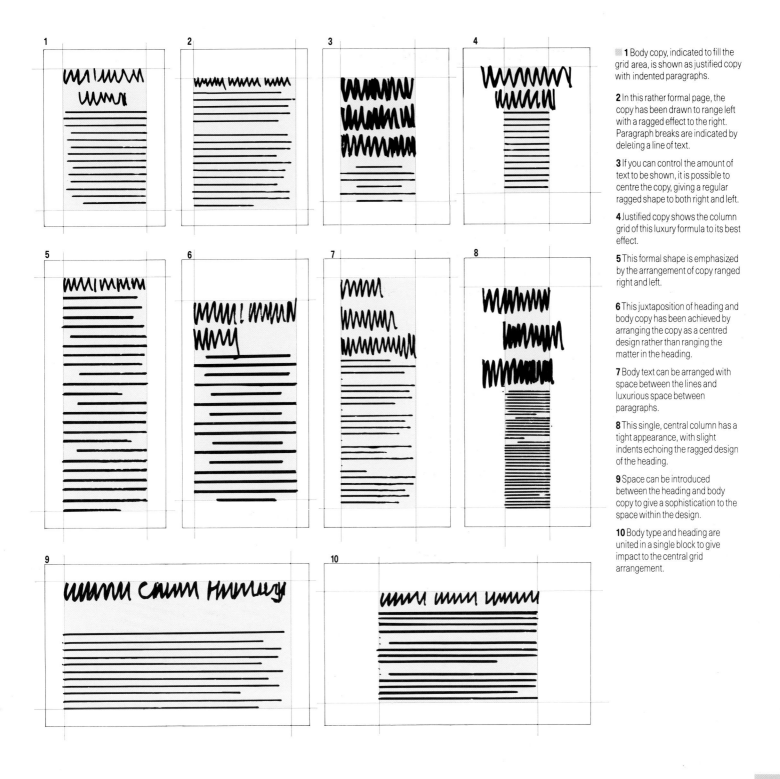

1 Body copy, indicated to fill the grid area, is shown as justified copy with indented paragraphs.

2 In this rather formal page, the copy has been drawn to range left with a ragged effect to the right. Paragraph breaks are indicated by deleting a line of text.

3 If you can control the amount of text to be shown, it is possible to centre the copy, giving a regular ragged shape to both right and left.

4 Justified copy shows the column grid of this luxury formula to its best effect.

5 This formal shape is emphasized by the arrangement of copy ranged right and left.

6 This juxtaposition of heading and body copy has been achieved by arranging the copy as a centred design rather than ranging the matter in the heading.

7 Body text can be arranged with space between the lines and luxurious space between paragraphs.

8 This single, central column has a tight appearance, with slight indents echoing the ragged design of the heading.

9 Space can be introduced between the heading and body copy to give a sophistication to the space within the design.

10 Body type and heading are united in a single block to give impact to the central grid arrangement.

1

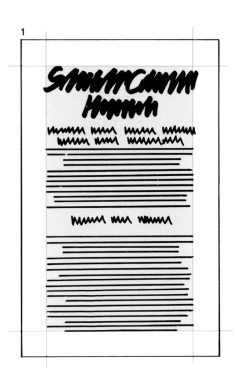

2

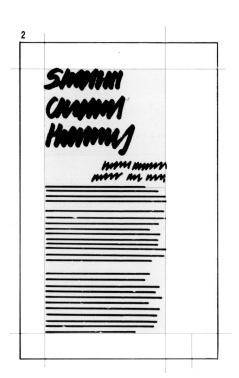

3

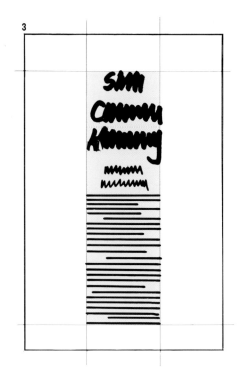

4

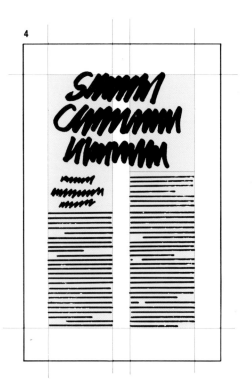

5

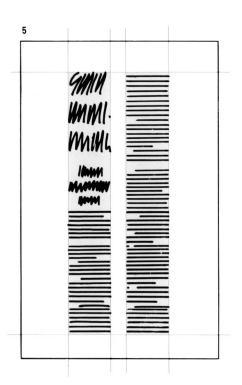

6

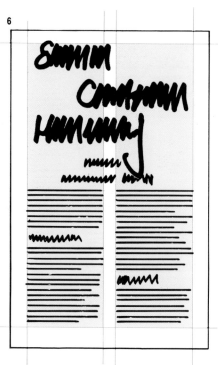

SUB-HEADINGS

Between the dynamic forces of headings and body copy, you will find a need for another element. This is usually created by the natural inclusion of sub-headings, which are usually visually weighted somewhere between the body matter and the heading. They can be used to liven up the design and to create a patch-work appearance in the design effect. You should consider the weight of these elements carefully and try them out in different positions on the grid layout.

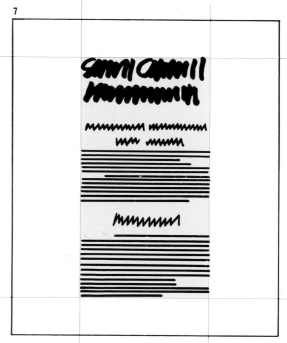

1 The sub-heading is used as a visual buffer between the heading and body text, and the second sub-heading is used to relieve the monotony of lengthy text.

2 Ranging the sub-heading right counterbalances the heading and body copy, which have been ranged left.

3 A centred sub-heading punctuates the space between heading and body copy.

4 An introductory sub-heading occupies a space equal to, and lining up with, the top of the second column, making the two columns into a formal, united block.

5 A condensed sub-heading halfway down the page acts as a visual buffer between the heading and the start of the body copy.

6 A centred sub-heading, with secondary sub-headings ranged between the copy acting as visual pauses.

7 Sub-headings can be used as design devices to separate solid body text.

8 Sub-headings that are ranged right counteract the informality of the heading design.

9 The first sub-heading is used as the formal introduction to the body copy, while a second is used as a design device.

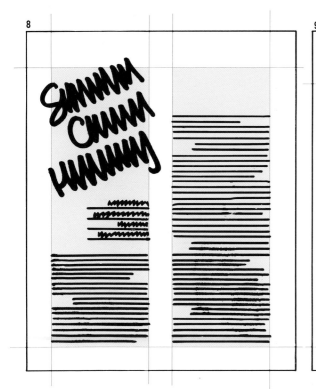

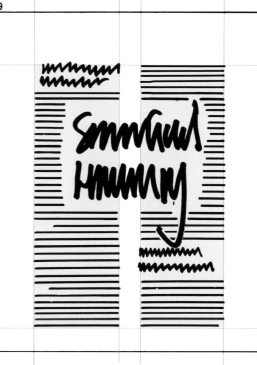

CHECKLIST

- Introduce body copy to the headings on your thumbnail sketches of the grids.
- Indicate the body copy, using different weights of line for different typefaces.
- Render the heading and body copy to achieve a complementary balance.
- Stay within the grid guidelines.
- Introduce sub-headings as an intermediate force.

Headings, body copy and pictures

DESIGNING A LAYOUT will quite often include the use of pictures of some kind, and these elements will add a completely new dimension to your work. In these early pages, using the one-column and two-column grids only, you will see how these elements can be manipulated in many different ways. Gaining a basic understanding of the design variations that are possible on this limited scale will prepare you to try some more adventurous ideas.

The dynamics of this new element – pictures – give you scope to break out of the formal restraints created by the typographic elements. Pictures can be used instantly in a more flexible and stimulating way than you have so far been allowed. They can break across columns and into margins, disregarding the confines of the page layout. Some pictures can be formulated as shapes, and the body text can then be arranged to form a shape around the picture.

Assessing the picture itself and its intrinsic interest, use your creative and visual judgement to decide how large and powerful its presence is to be within the layout. Produce a number of alternative layouts with different sized pictures to discover how the proportions of the elements relate to one another and to the grid. The headings and sub-headings can be used to counterbalance the effect of visual weight within the design, and body text should be considered as a tonal contrast in your design.

Pictures can be used as tones of black and white or, if colour is available, they can be used to give creative and interesting visual variations, but at this stage of the work you should be looking, albeit in abstract terms, at the contrast of the characteristics of the design elements.

By reducing or enlarging the picture or pictures, and even by trying different shape formats against various sizes of text, you will begin to make some alternative design decisions without great difficulty.

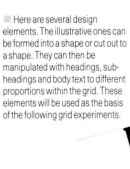

Here are several design elements. The illustrative ones can be formed into a shape or cut out to a shape. They can then be manipulated with headings, sub-headings and body text to different proportions within the grid. These elements will be used as the basis of the following grid experiments.

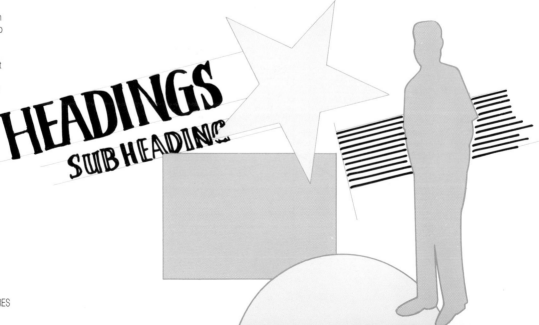

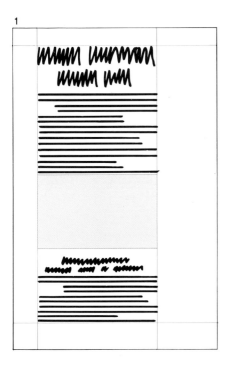

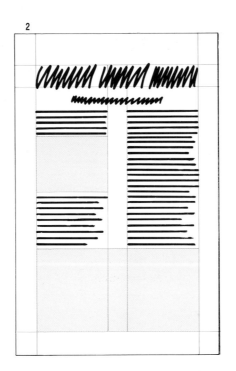

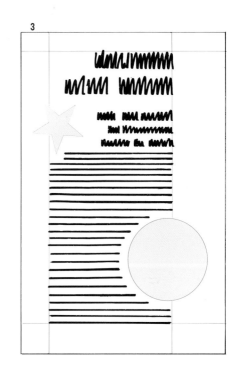

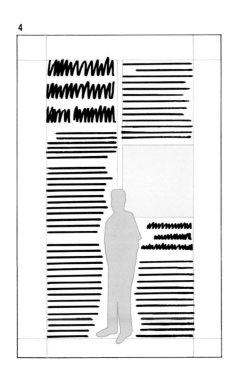

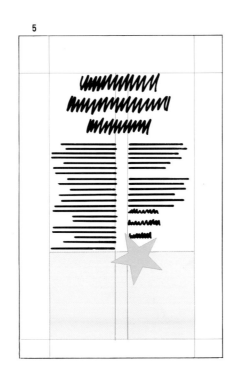

■ **1** A simple, squared-off picture sits firmly between the grid margins, positioned slightly below the centre of the page.

2 Two squared-off pictures are used here, one arranged over a single column to break up the body copy, and the second over two columns to form a base for the design.

3 Pictures can be used to liven up a formal arrangement, breaking in and out of the grid.

4 Formal and informal shapes link and overlap. The informal shape is used to break up the two rigid columns.

5 An informal shape breaks into a squared-off picture, sitting across the two columns but running off the bottom of the design area.

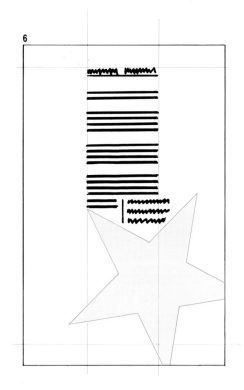

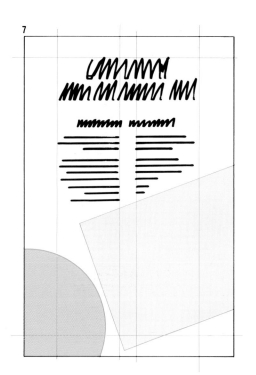

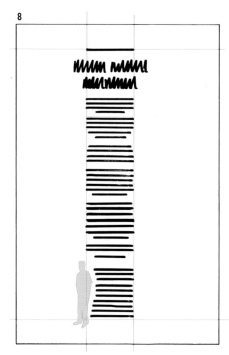

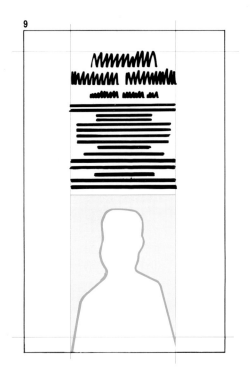

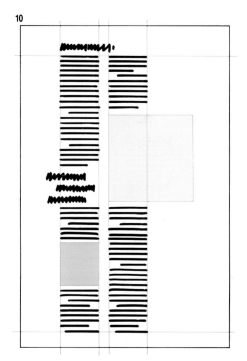

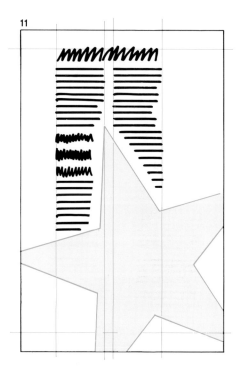

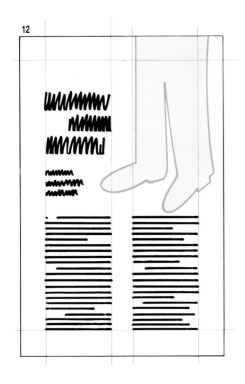

12

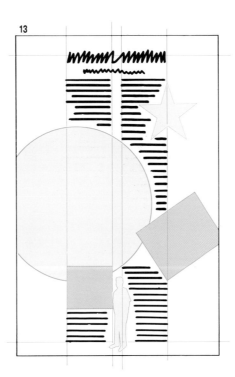

13

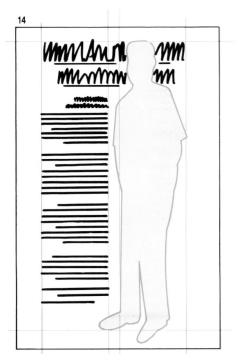

14

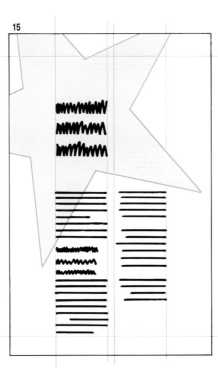

15

6 An informal shape used outside the constraints of a formal single column has a dynamic effect.

7 Shapes, both informal and formal, can be used without regard for the formality of the grid.

8 The subtle non-conformity of scale is shown by the cut-out picture, which has been overpowered by towering headings and body text.

9 Tone is used here, squared off behind the cut-out picture.

10 Squared-off pictures are used to create visual tension.

11 A dynamic shape breaks off the page on both sides and at the bottom, while secondary shapes are formed with body copy.

12 This informal shape serves as a lead in to the headings and body copy.

13 Random shapes are used to create a pattern within and outside the grid.

14 A heading and cut-out shape are linked, the shape balancing with the body copy, which forms a two-column grid.

15 The heading and text run over a cut-out shape in the background.

CHECKLIST

- Place the picture in outline form on a thumbnail of your grid.
- Try the picture at different visual proportions.
- Try breaking the convention of the grid.
- Fill in your sketches with solid tone or colours to compare the balance of image.
- Try alternatives, using solid shapes to represent the pictorial elements.

1 This scamp for a double-page spread shows a five-column grid, with the elements arranged dynamically over the grids and central gutter. Copy has been scamped at two-column and single-column width. This initial stage gives scope for various interpretations of the layout using the same elements.

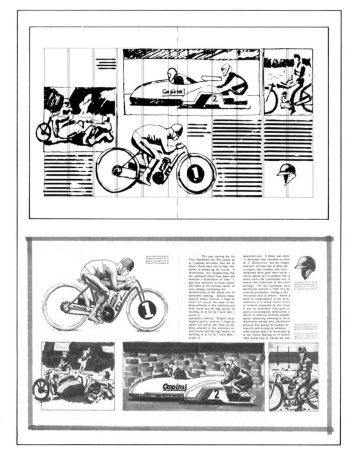

2 The finished design no longer conspicuously uses the five columns, although the five-column grid is very much in evidence below the surface. Tonally, the weight of the layout is stressed across the bottom third of the design area.

THE FLEXIBILITY OF GRIDS

ONCE YOU HAVE ESTABLISHED the relevance of a grid and the ways in which exciting and interesting design decisions can be influenced by this compositional device, you can enter the next phase of understanding. So far, we have looked at a few simple shapes, representing graphic elements, manipulated within the simple grid structures shown. You have seen how the proportions are adjustable within this framework, and you have discovered how elements can be given different priorities, albeit in an abstract form, by using different tones. The design space should always be viewed in the way one would view an empty room. Such a room would have different degrees of depth, which can be broken by the shape and proportions of objects placed within it. Similarly, your design area has the same potential, and, although I am referring to a flat, two-dimensional surface, you will find this other dimension if you remember to regard this space in terms of depth.

In this section of the book you will see how the compositional device – the grid – can be manipulated to segment the design area into new and original formats. By splitting columns into further divisions and arranging elements to conform to these proportions, you are able to run two grids of different sizes within a single design. This aspect of grids opens up a whole new concept in the design approach. You are able to change the measurements of typesetting and create a tension and atmosphere within the typographic elements.

Columns can be divided into margins. If the grid is divided, these margins can be used as areas in which all manner of invention can take place. Small illustrations can be floated in these areas. Captions can break up the space with a rhythmic use of type. Heavy single letter forms can be dropped into place, and, if you choose, tints or colour can be applied. In effect, the flexibility of the surface space becomes a design element to be exploited.

You should still remember my earlier point about the proportion and tonal effect of this surface while you are now able to consider the surface compositional arrangement.

On the following pages you will see how the design elements can be arranged and a different design formula achieved by choosing different grid arrangements. You will see how styling can be affected by subtle choices of grid compositions and by the use of the elements within those compositions. In addition, the elements themselves can be changed and explored to provide contrast in design.

Grid options

NOW THAT YOU UNDERSTAND the principles of using a grid you can start to look at the design options made possible by the chosen grid. Before proceeding any further, though, I should mention the client, for it is the client who will dictate some of the visual parameters of the design. The brief that you have received from your client will contain some key pointers to the way you are to begin. Consider the brief together with the function and purpose of the design you are going to create. I mention this because some designs will be one-off projects, while others will be on-going. The single design job will probably require less forward thinking and a more inspirational use of the grid; the on-going print project, on the other hand, will need a common structure that can relate to each commission as it arises.

Some projects will need a grid only in the early part of the design process, whereas others may need pre-printed grid sheets for subsequent work. This aspect of grid design will be discussed later.

You will discover that you can divide the design area into as many columns as you wish. However, remember that the columns will be used mostly for body copy and that, therefore, practicalities regarding the realistic width of these should be foremost in your mind. A three-column grid would traditionally be considered a good option in brochure work. This gives you wide, readable columns of type and the added flexibility of being able to split them further into six columns. This arrangement works even more effectively when it is opened out into a double-page spread, which gives you the option of a range between six and twelve columns over the entire area.

This formula, together with the two-column division, which can be easily adjusted to four columns, is the most commonly applied grid formula. The reason for this is quite simple. An even number of columns enables the designer to keep a balanced and even spread on the page, although this is restrictive in itself and can result in fairly ordinary and unimaginative layouts.

On the other hand, grids with an uneven number of columns, such as five, seven or odd and even numbers of columns on facing spreads, will give a different styling to the overall concept. I hope you now begin to see the importance of actually designing a range of grids, as thumbnail sketches, before you begin the design project.

1 The traditional three-column grid formula, which is ideally suited for magazine design, is shown here as a three-column grid, further sub-divided into six columns.

2 Two columns create a fairly heavy, academic quality; they are easily divided into four columns.

3 The five-column grid gives you great flexibility in arranging type over two columns, leaving a single column that can float and be used as a design device.

4 The seven-column grid offers even greater flexibility, and many combinations can be explored, leaving one or two columns as floating graphic devices.

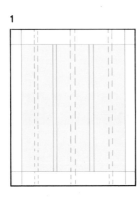

1

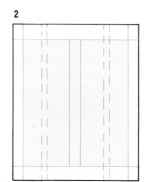

2

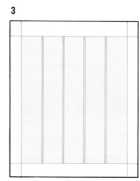

3

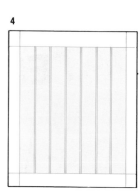

4

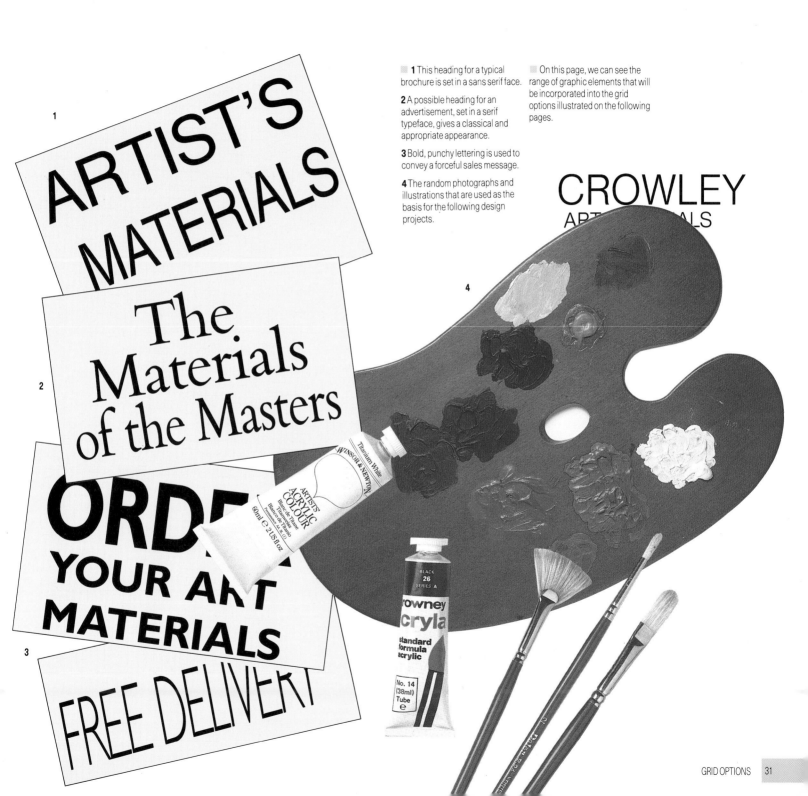

1 This heading for a typical brochure is set in a sans serif face.

2 A possible heading for an advertisement, set in a serif typeface, gives a classical and appropriate appearance.

3 Bold, punchy lettering is used to convey a forceful sales message.

4 The random photographs and illustrations that are used as the basis for the following design projects.

On this page, we can see the range of graphic elements that will be incorporated into the grid options illustrated on the following pages.

1

ARTIST'S MATERIALS

2

The Materials of the Masters

3

ORDER YOUR ART MATERIALS

FREE DELIVERY

4

CROWLEY
ART MATERIALS

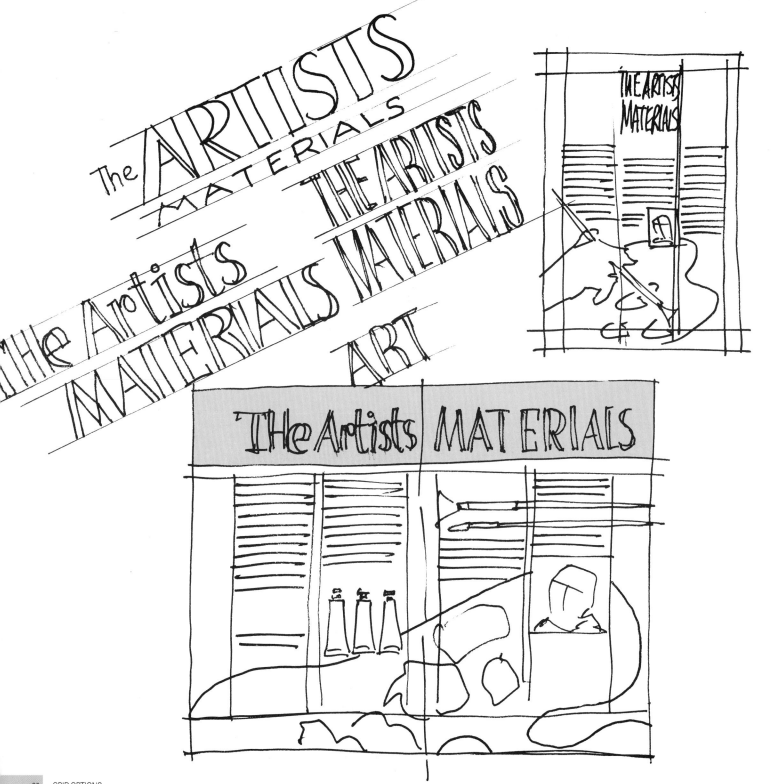

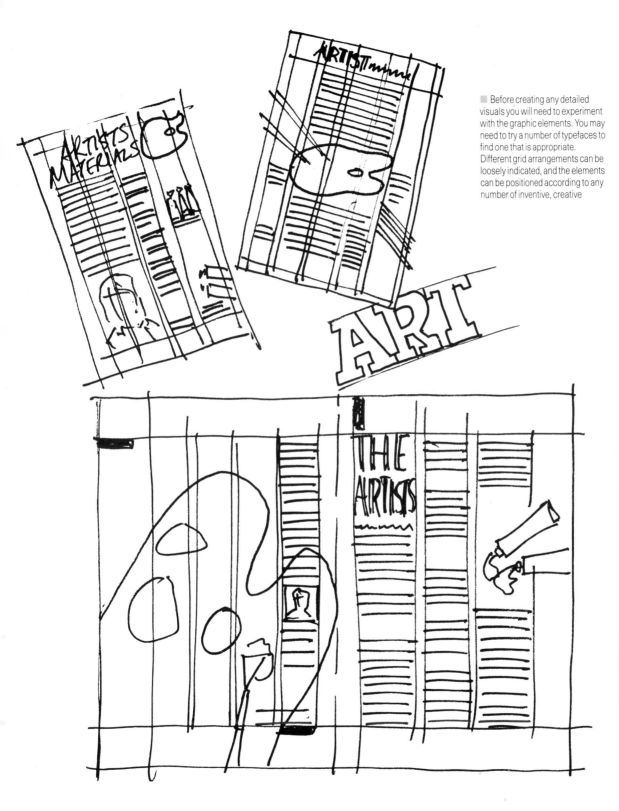

Before creating any detailed visuals you will need to experiment with the graphic elements. You may need to try a number of typefaces to find one that is appropriate. Different grid arrangements can be loosely indicated, and the elements can be positioned according to any number of inventive, creative formulae. Different weights of type can be hinted at, but if there is extensive copy, you will need to have some idea of how much space it is likely to occupy. The two small examples will give you some idea of how space and the number of words are affected by the size and proportions of the type.

This example shows 8 point type set within an 11 point space.

The first principle of good design is a grid. The first principle of good design is a grid. The first principle of good design is a grid. The first principle of good design is a grid. The first principle of good design is a

This example shows 9 point setting with no extra space; this is known as 9 point set solid.

The first principle of good design is a grid. The first principle of good design is a grid. The first principle of good design is a grid. The first principle of good design is a grid. The first principle of good design is a grid. The first

CHECKLIST

- Work out how your grid can divide into more columns.

- Produce as many alternatives as you can.

- Produce a number of thumbnail sketches using imaginary graphic elements to see how the alternatives work.

- Draw the elements loosely in pencil and the grids themselves in light blue.

Three-column and six-column grids

THE THREE-COLUMN GRID can often be found underlying magazines, newsletters and some advertising material. It is a common format, one that is safe but unadventurous. If squared-off pictures are placed on this format, they will normally be placed in the width of a single column to punctuate copy without intruding too much on the page. However, with imagination you are still able to break the visual code of this grid. Advertisers often use this formula when they display a large picture at the top of the page across the three columns and lightly display limited information at the foot. This information at the foot often carries a product logo, which may be off-set from the confines of the grid.

This display is actually very cunning. Your attention is drawn to the formality of the positioning of the picture, while the logo, which contrasts with the formality, catches your eye through its unconventionality in breaking the composition. The body text is left in its formal space for you to read once your attention is caught. This type of arrangement can be exploited in a wide range of different situations.

In conclusion, although three-column grids can produce extremely formal layouts, these need not become tedious if you include a subtle twist to the convention of the design.

It is simple to create six columns in the range of grids that can be based on three columns. This arrangement would not be appropriate for the body copy for an average design job because the type would have to be too small to be arranged satisfactorily and legibly within the column width. However, there will be certain occasions when you can use this number of columns for text. One of these circumstances would be for a list of names; another would be in a catalogue, where captions are used to support pictures. This method of dividing the design space can be used very effectively when there is more visual matter than text. Occasionally, alternating between three and six columns on adjacent pages can create an interesting visual balance.

Finally, although the underlying composition may be over three or six columns, you do not, of course, have to fill all of these columns with visual elements. In fact, it is sometimes desirable, when you have the luxury of limited text and effective pictures, simply to run a single column of text and to break it with a stunning picture. This allows the space around these elements to work as a design feature in its own right.

Explore a range of different three-column grid sizes to find the appropriate format for the project in hand. For single design jobs, the grid can be less conventional and offer scope for originality.

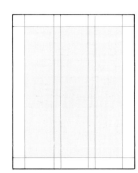
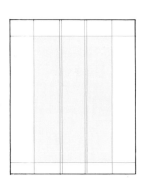
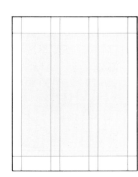

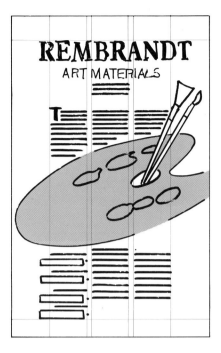

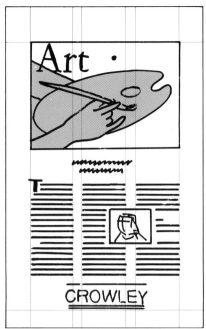

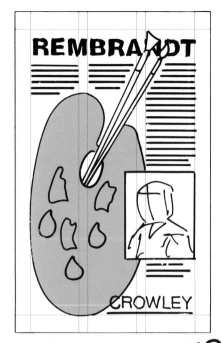

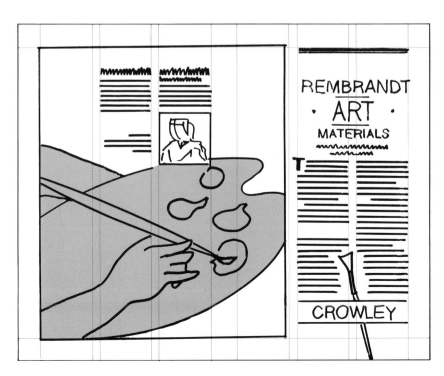

THE ARTIST'S MATERIALS
The Materials of the Masters

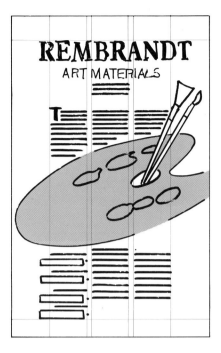 **Above** A number of typefaces showing the different visual emphasis you can give to the headings.

On this page you can see a number of ideas that explore the basic three-column grid formula. The basic grid can be divided to give more flexibility, as can be seen in the second example at the top of the page. Notice how the capital letters at the beginning of the copy can be enlarged to add some design refinement.

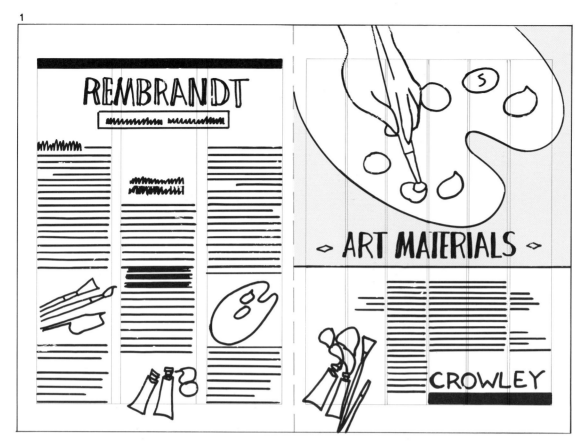

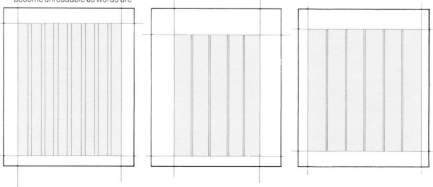

1 Combining two grids within a design area is an effective way of changing the emphasis of the information displayed. In this design, the three-column grid carries the bulk of the copy, which has been only slightly interrupted with small picture breaks. The six-column grid gives scope to create a busy and visually less formal arrangement of the elements.

Six-column grids divide the design area into an even pattern of narrow strips. Make sure that these individual spaces do not become too restrictive for effective typesetting – the text could easily become unreadable as words are split and carried over to the next line. Six columns are often used for listing addresses if companies have many branches or outlets to display on a page. Try a number of different visual arrangements.

2

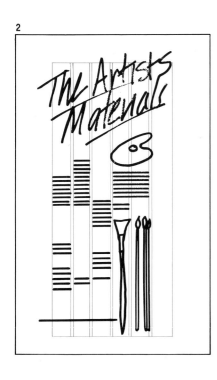

3

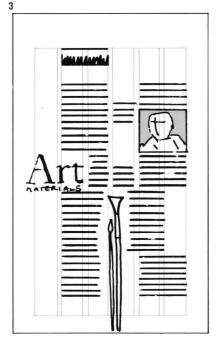

4

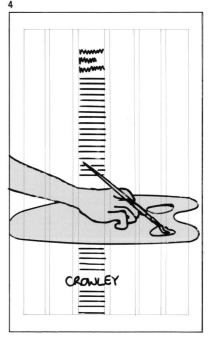

5

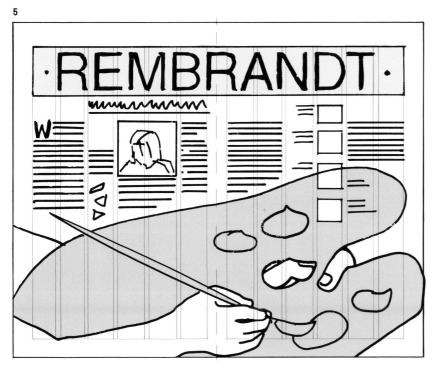

■ **2** The six slim columns give an elegant, condensed feel to the design elements displayed within this space.

3 The grid has been used so that the central area contains two columns of double-column setting and two single columns. This has been broken by the heading, which is informally displayed to the left, while the brush illustration intrudes from the bottom of the page.

4 One of the six columns can be used to dynamic effect, with the picture breaking the entire design area.

5 Twelve columns, or the arrangement of two six-column pages, gives scope for great flexibility. Two columns, joined to carry copy, can be punctuated by single-column spaces, and large and small pictorial elements can be counterbalanced to create effective displays.

CHECKLIST

■ Draw the design area as an outline.

■ Draw a number of three- and six-column arrangements in light blue pen.

■ Choose a picture and some text at random.

■ Imagine the picture at different proportions and sizes within the grid.

■ Arrange the text in several different ways around the pictorial elements.

■ Remember that text can be produced in different sizes and typefaces; these will give different stresses to the layout.

■ Pay special attention to the layout of the larger type such as headings, sub-headings and logos.

Two-column and four-column grids

THESE TRADITIONAL FORMULAE allow considerable flexibility, as the two-column grid can stand on its own to any given size within the design space, or it can be subdivided to create four columns. This is flexible because, when the area is divided into four columns, it is easy not to use one column for design elements and so to leave a broad margin to counter-balance the text. The text itself can always be typeset to create tension on the page simply by setting one of the columns of type in a heavier typeface than the adjacent columns.

Remember that, although the grid is divided into equal measurements, these need not completely fill the page. It is always desirable to allow space around this compositional area, and, whenever you can, you should seek the opportunity to include space as a factor in your design. Having said this, you will know just how far you can go if you know your client. For instance, if your client is a magazine editor, he may be more concerned with the printed word than with the design. The same would apply to a cost-conscious company manager who is buying advertising space; he will want to show his superiors that he has obtained value for money. But your job as a designer is also to educate your client into a realization of the subtleties and distinctiveness that come from allowing scope for space within the design project.

Two- and four-column grids can be used with great distinction. Strategically placing a nice balance of design and illustrative elements enables you to create both formal and informal layouts. When double spreads are a feature of the design, you can picture this as eight columns in total, or subdivide them in all manner of ways, using perhaps two of the columns on one page and three on the other. This allows interesting spaces for you to experiment with the other elements.

▨ Once again there are many alternatives open with the two- and four-column grids. You should consider the priorities of the visual elements that you are going to display, bearing in mind that two columns on a broad measure will give you a classical, academic appearance, while four columns will enable you to display text in a lighter and more contemporary style, so that the text can be interspersed with different weights of type matter.

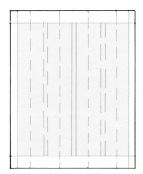
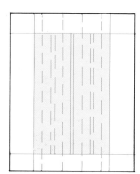
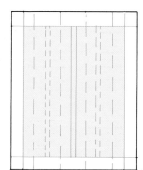
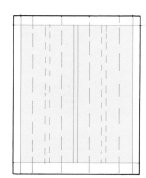

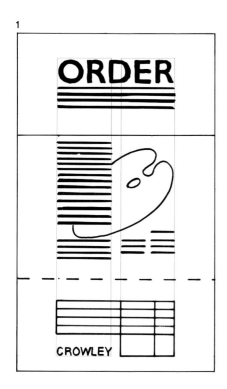

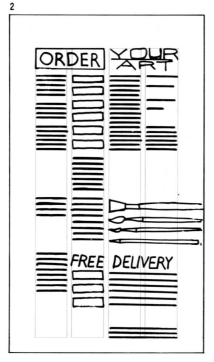

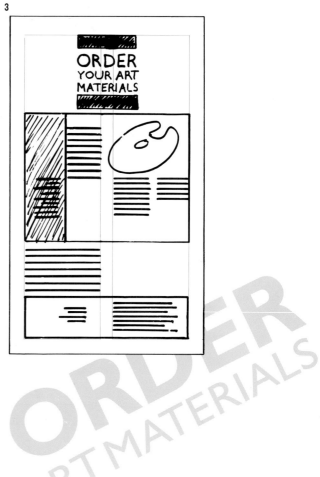

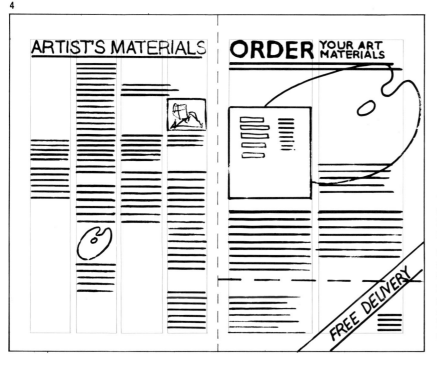

1 This design for a leaflet uses two of the columns to display a single column of text, while the less important text is displayed in a narrow, single column.

2 The body copy is displayed according to the four-column formula, while the bolder typographic messages are displayed over the two adjoining columns. This has the effect of locking the centre of the layout within a solid structure.

3 Information is displayed over the width of the grid, and the text is separated into two single columns. The heading is arranged to the width of the single column, but centred on the design.

4 A combination of four columns facing two columns gives the design area two distinctive visual arrangements for the messages to be displayed.

Right Within this single design it has been possible to mix a number of grid options. On the left there is a four-column grid, headed by a two-column central graphic device. On the right-hand page, the grid has been further divided into thirds, the first of these sub-divisions displaying a four-column arrangement. Alongside, the same area is divided into a single-column width. Below this, the four-column grid has been further divided into one- and three-column areas.

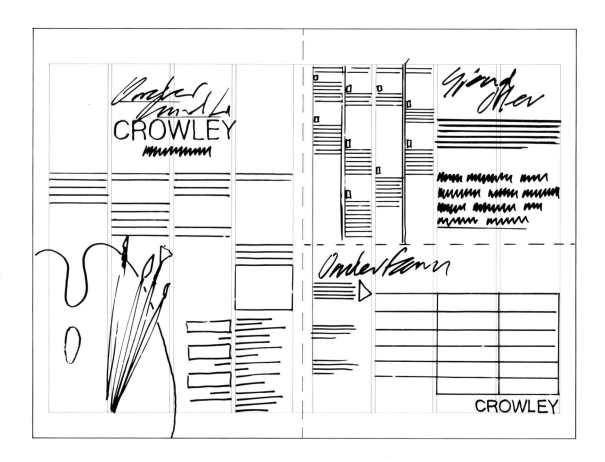

Below You can comfortably divide four columns into eight. The eight columns are probably far too narrow for single columns of text and are more likely to be useful in the creation of a flexible design.

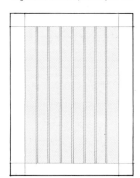
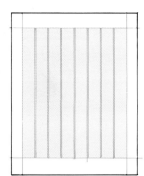

1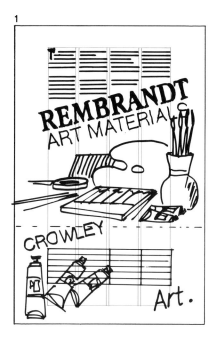

2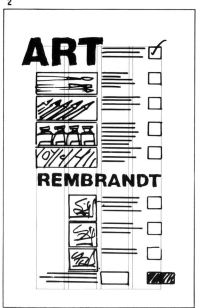

3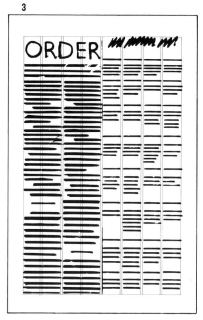

4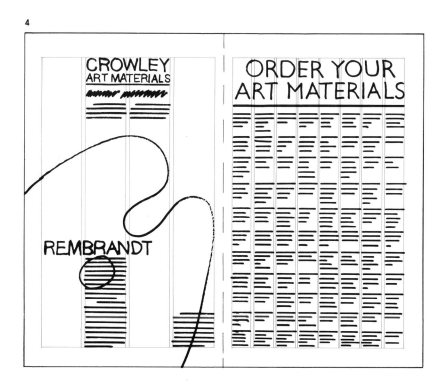

■ **1, 2, 3 & 4** A variety of design options using four columns as the fundamental base to the design can be seen here, with further exploration of the possibilities of using eight columns. Although not practical for body copy, they could be used for listing references, addresses, price lists and so on.

CHECKLIST

- ■ Produce some thumbnails of different two- and four-column formats.

- ■ Think about the margin space and space between columns.

- ■ Try some alternative spacings at top and bottom.

- ■ Indicate the body text, giving a different creative feel to each layout.

- ■ Try some double-page arrangements with different numbers of columns.

- ■ Test the effect you can create by leaving space.

Mixing grid formats

THERE ARE MANY WAYS of creating visual tension within the design space. The first of these is to arrange the design elements in a manner that creates compositional stresses within the design. What I mean by this is that, by reducing and enlarging the components through various proportional balances and imbalances, ideas for the most effective formula will emerge.

Although this makes a play on the underlying grid, the design is still dictated by the initial decision. One method of deliberately achieving this design tension and of creating unusual balances and stresses within the design area is to create a situation in which these effects are forced upon the design area. This allows the design elements to be placed more flexibly within the column arrangement.

For instance, a five-column grid format has been developed for this book, yet, you will say, there are only two columns of text, with a wide margin on the right- and left-hand sides of the page. This is because each column of text occupies two of the column divisions, leaving one further column to float on the page. This column allows space on the outer edge for additional information – you will find checklists and captions in this space. Occasionally you will even identify the five columns by the way the pictures have been positioned. This arrangement gives the book a smart and spacious feel, with the added bonus of an outer margin for you to make notes in – hence the term the "scholar's margin".

For a book grid I could have decided to have five columns on one side of a double-page spread and four on the other. Alternatively, I could have chosen three and two columns, or three and four, or even five and eight.

Here you can see a sample page from this book. The space has, as you can see, been divided into five columns, with the text set to two columns, which are placed across four of the grid columns, leaving a luxurious-looking margin to the outer edge. Drawings below the text and the captions occupy the four inner columns. On the opposite page the drawings are made to fit within the overall grid shape, although they do not relate directly to the column measures.

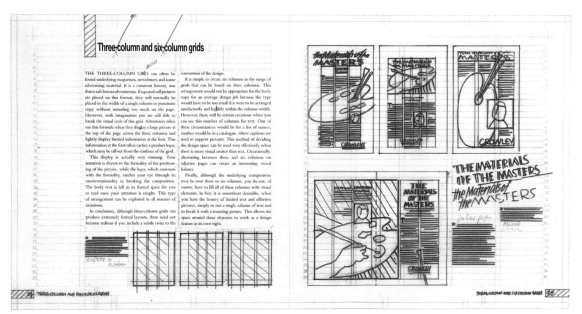

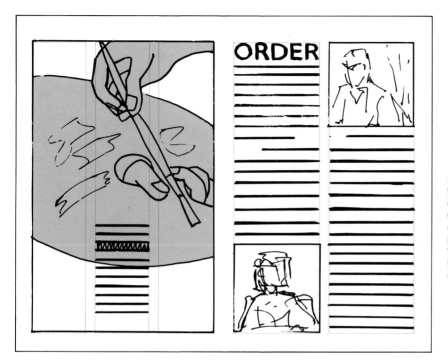

**The South East Essex
College of Arts & Technology**
Carnarvon Road   Southend on Sea   Essex   SS2 6LS
Tel: Southend (0702) 220400   Fax: Southend (0702) 432320

Left A mixture of three- and two-column displays. The three-column layout is useful for overlaying photographs if a central column of text is lifted out of the photograph. The two-column format forms a solid, informative-looking block that complements the area of the photograph.

Right Five and six columns can be used to separate the design elements. The five-column grid divides comfortably into two wide columns, allowing a marginal column for sub-headings and additional information. The six columns can be used with dynamic flexibility for the display of the technical, graphic elements.

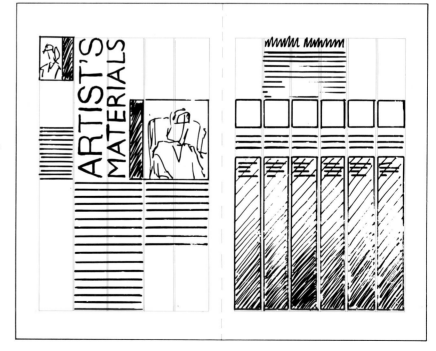

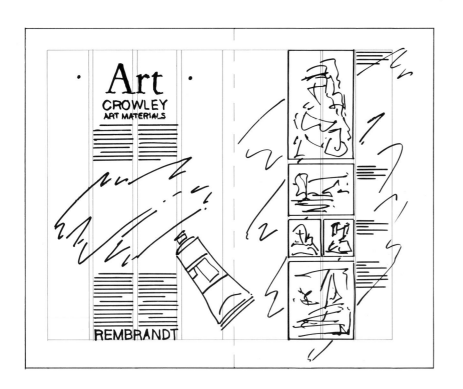

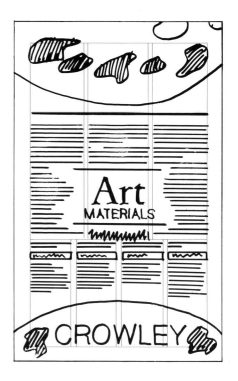

Do not impose constraints on the design. It is quite acceptable to mix grids within a single design area, where a number of combinations may be used. Modern typographic technology makes it possible to create interesting shapes with the type itself.

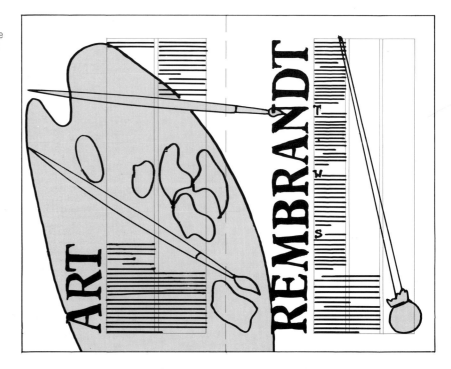

Whatever juxtaposition of grid formats you use, you will discover that certain compositional decisions will become obvious. I suggest that you experiment extensively with these as thumbnail sketches to see what is possible. Even if one of your pages is completely covered with a photograph or illustration, you should still use a grid to underpin the layout. Then, if some text or just a heading appears in conjunction with the image, it will be underpinned by the grid design. This is where subtleties within the composition can be produced, and it is also a great opportunity to introduce another grid format.

The fascination of designing with a grid derives from its final invisibility. Like an architectural structure, the grid represents the bricks and mortar, and the decorative features are the graphic elements. When you look at a building you perceive its design more often than its structure. This concept applies to designing with grids, when the final image seen is merely the graphic adornment.

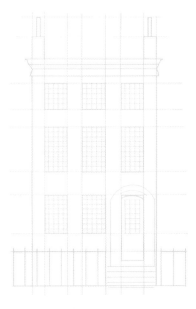

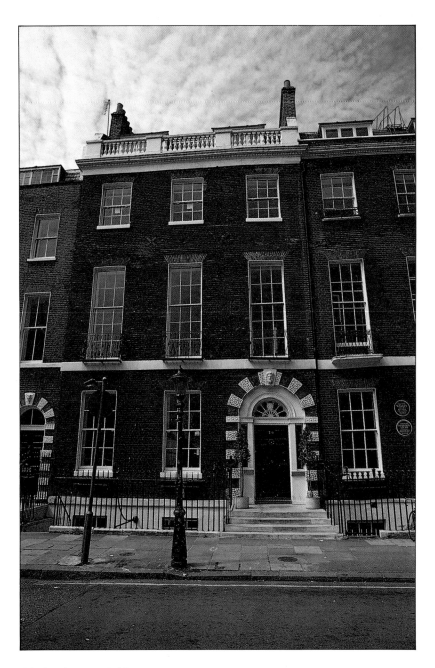

■ Look at this photograph of the building and the line drawing to establish an idea of the design's compositional structure.

1 to 6 The seven-column format is a flexible basis for many design options. It gives you a great number of attractive possibilities by combining columns into different width arrangements. A two/four/one combination, in which the single remains blank, gives you the scholar's margin. You can see from the drawings that there are a number of alternatives in which the single free column is indicated with a tint. Try out a number of layouts for yourself using this seven-column structure as a base.

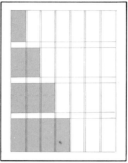

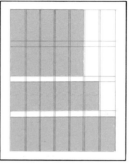

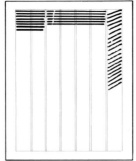

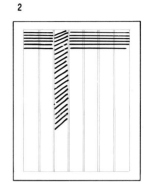

The seven-column arrangement gives you many options for sub-dividing the area, for the visual matter can extend from one to seven columns. The height of the picture can vary as much as the width, although you may need to work out a proportional, uniform size to strike a happy balance between pictures and text.

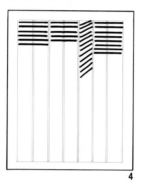

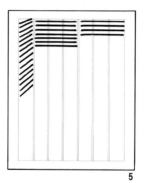

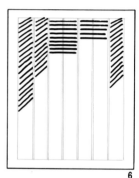

3

4

5

6

7

7 For innovative design there is no reason why the grid should remain in a vertical position. A tilt of, say, 30 degrees will change the entire visual force of the information displayed. Alternatively, you can keep the columns vertical but tilt the information at set degrees. This would require a separate grid, which should be drawn up at this angle to align the visual elements.

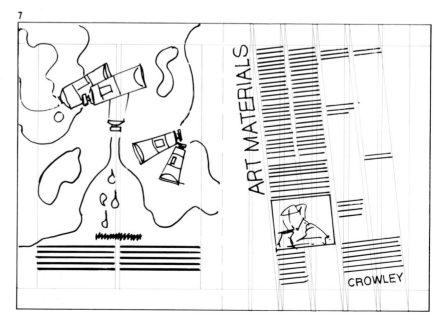

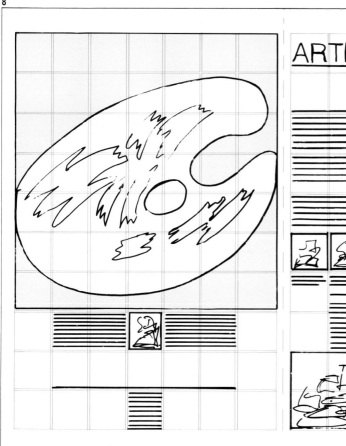

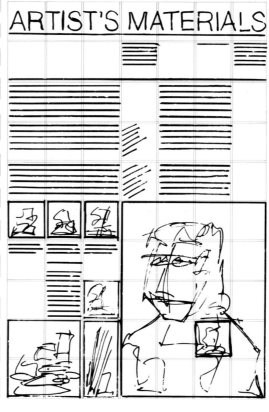

8

ARTIST'S MATERIALS

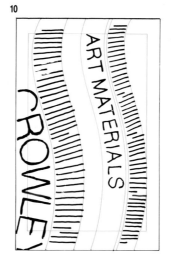

8 For more complex geometric design, for which the grid will work vertically and horizontally, you will need to draw up a segmented structure to accommodate your ideas not only for the design and the design elements, but also for your experiments. It is possible, with this format, to subdivide the area into separate compositions that occupy their own design modules.

9 It is possible to create a modular grid that will give you different design options within a structured format. The grid itself makes certain visual implications so that the designer has an expressive framework within which to work.

10 Experimenting with curves may also reveal a successful way to underpin your grid. This may give you an expressive and unusual base for the display of the graphic elements.

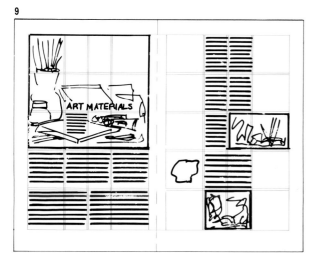

9

CHECKLIST

- Draw a number of uneven column grids as thumbnail sketches.

- Try out your graphic elements in different ways on these grids.

- See how the space left by unused columns can give you interesting effects.

- Try different grid arrangements for each page on double-page spreads.

- Try various alternatives.

- Indicate a full-page photograph on one spread and see how you can move a heading around in this space.

- Erase the grid lines to see the design you have created.

The grid in the design process

THE FIRST STEP in the design process is to establish the brief. A meeting with your client to discuss the design requirements is essential. You will discover how much copy is to be included in the design, and you may even receive the manuscript of the text at this point. You will determine the importance of headings and sub-headings, discuss the visual components, such as photographs or illustrations, and, more importantly, you will get an idea of the client's preferences with regard to styling, for the client will certainly wish to express his or her opinion on the image for the design. You must also not neglect to discuss the budget allocated to the job, as this will affect every stage, including the type of illustration you will be able to afford.

STARTING WORK

The first decision must be the grid format. Establish this by producing thumbnail sketches to show a variety of grid arrangements within different shapes. These can be drawn lightly in pencil or blue pen. Once a possible range of grids has emerged, you can begin to acquaint yourself with the graphic information that must be incorporated into the design. If there is an abundance of space, your first consideration is to work out how your text will fit. When you have no experience, the simplest way is to draw the layout up to full size to establish the space for text. Then in magazines find text of different sizes and styles, and choose the one most suitable for your layout. Cut out the text to fit your layout areas. Place the cut-out text in position, then count the number of characters and word spaces in one line and multiply this by the total number of lines used. This gives you the number of characters fitting the space in this size of type. A character count of your manuscript establishes how these compare and if larger or smaller type is needed. Next, show the appropriate example of typesetting to the printer as he will make the necessary final calculations.

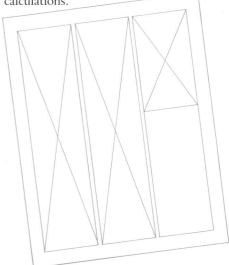

■ When the design involves a large amount of body copy, the measurements of the grid need to be established first so that the type area can be calculated accurately.

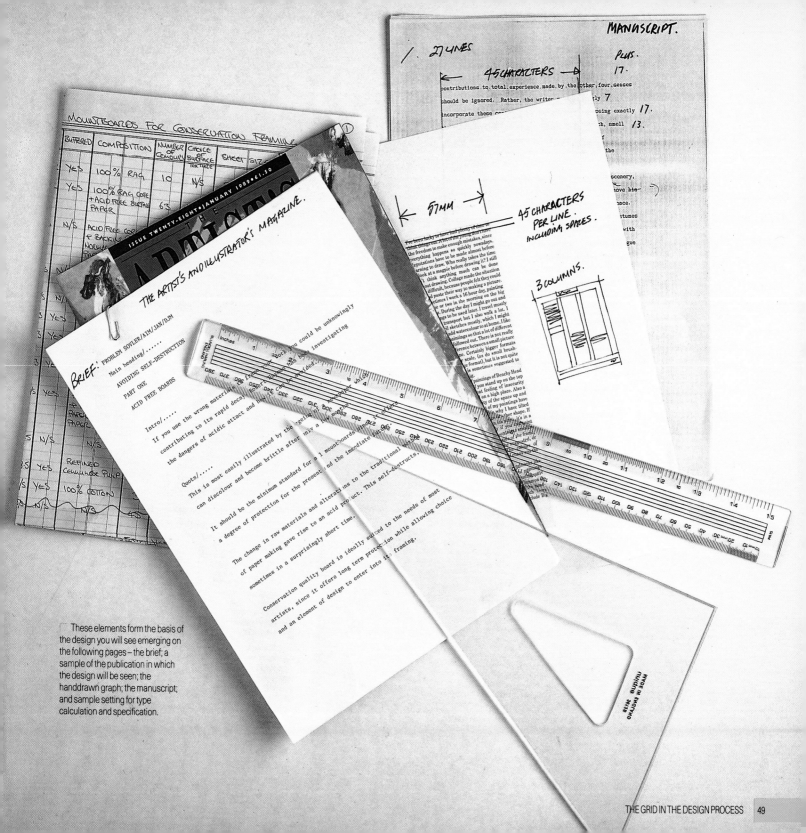

These elements form the basis of the design you will see emerging on the following pages – the brief; a sample of the publication in which the design will be seen; the handdrawn graph; the manuscript; and sample setting for type calculation and specification.

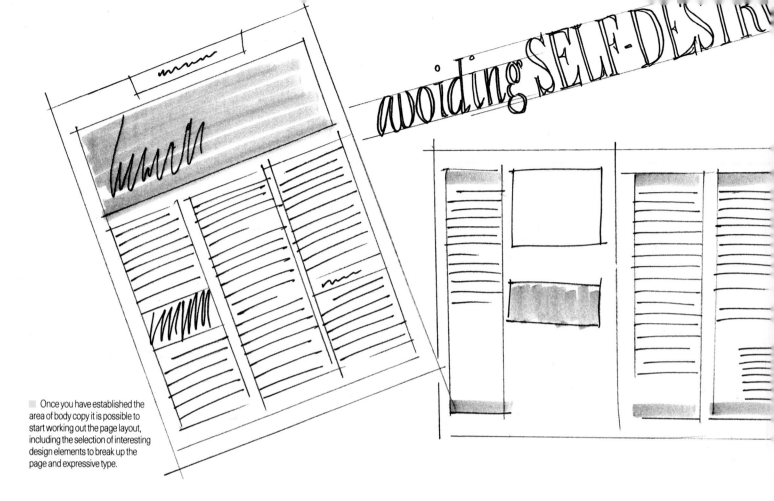

avoiding SELF-DESTR

Once you have established the area of body copy it is possible to start working out the page layout, including the selection of interesting design elements to break up the page and expressive type.

Once this laborious process has been completed you can move to the more interesting aspects, armed with the knowledge that the text will occupy a certain percentage of the total design area.

The real designing starts now that you can move around your text, creating different shapes and formats, using headings in different styles and sizes and producing ideas for photographs or illustrations that will give pictorial stress to the overall layout. You may also include design devices such as those found on the pages of this book, where strips of tint lead in from the head and foot of the page, and coloured squares have been subtly dropped into the captions to make a design feature of these elements. Tints, lines, dots, dividing rules, underlining, slabs

of colour and many other ideas can be applied to your subject. You may even wish to reverse the entire image out of a single colour. Whatever you choose, however, the grid will still remain there to guide you through the design.

WORKING UP YOUR THUMBNAIL SKETCHES

You should begin with thumbnail sketches for two reasons. First, the thumbnails give you the freedom to express yourself quickly, without technical encumbrance, so that you can produce designs swiftly and economically. Second, creative freedom comes from the energy you can generate by working quickly.

Obviously, these thumbnails are the merest hint of what is yet to emerge. You will now begin to consider the design elements in their own right, and you will probably wish, for this purpose, to work to a larger format. I recommend that you do not work to full-size at this stage, unless the actual size is small enough for you to keep up the momentum of your speed of working. By now the design will itself be suggesting the preferred grid formats, and you should work your design ideas up on the basis of these intermediate sketches.

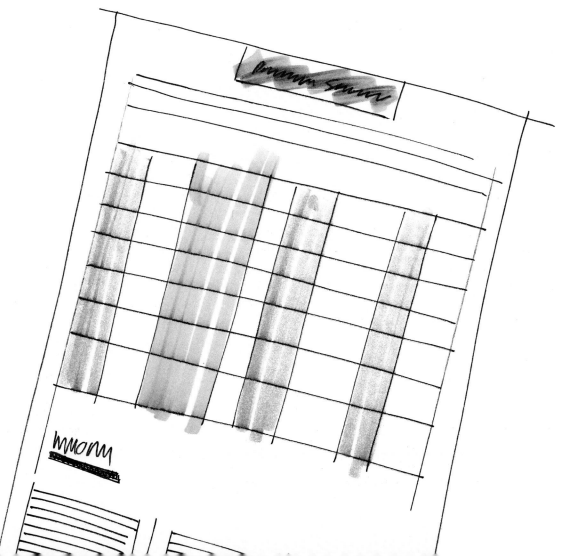

Even non-visual elements, such as the table of technical information, need to be designed to coordinate with the other pages as well as to communicate simply and effectively.

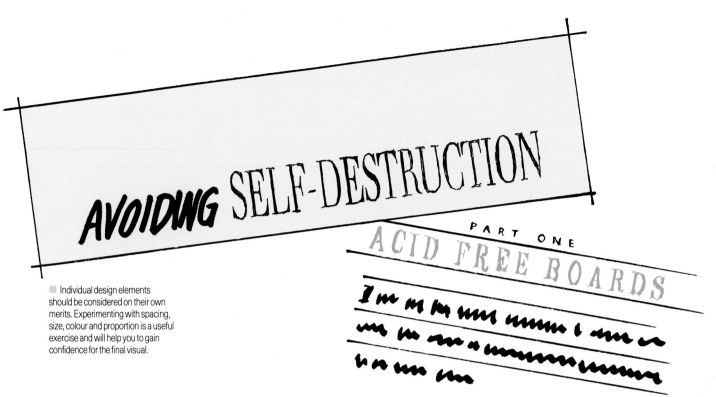

AVOIDING SELF-DESTRUCTION

PART ONE

ACID FREE BOARDS

■ Individual design elements should be considered on their own merits. Experimenting with spacing, size, colour and proportion is a useful exercise and will help you to gain confidence for the final visual.

It is at this point that you will spend some time assessing the distinctive visual values of different typefaces and experimenting with the subtleties that can be produced using colour, while looking at the range of illustration techniques and photographic images that could be applied to the design. You are, in effect, now in a position to see the differences between the designs emerging through the production of alternative layouts. These intermediate roughs can be used as the basis for a further meeting with your client if that is necessary.

PRODUCING VISUALS

Once you have had some feedback from your client, you can develop the suggestions that have emerged from your discussions. For a client presentation you may need to produce only one final visual to consolidate the design concept; this visual should resemble as closely as possible the final printed work and will most probably be produced to full size. The grid will not appear, of course; only the graphic imagery will be featured. All visuals used for client presentation will be prepared in this way, and if you remember to produce all your grids using an instrument that makes a mark that can be erased, it will be easier for you to display your work.

You may feel that your client needs to view more than one visual. This would mean that your finished visuals would be produced to a smaller scale than the finished size, both to help you in the production of this work and to restrict the expenses incurred.

On these pages you can see the entire process, from initial grid layouts produced as thumbnail sketches, through the emerging designs and to a final decision.

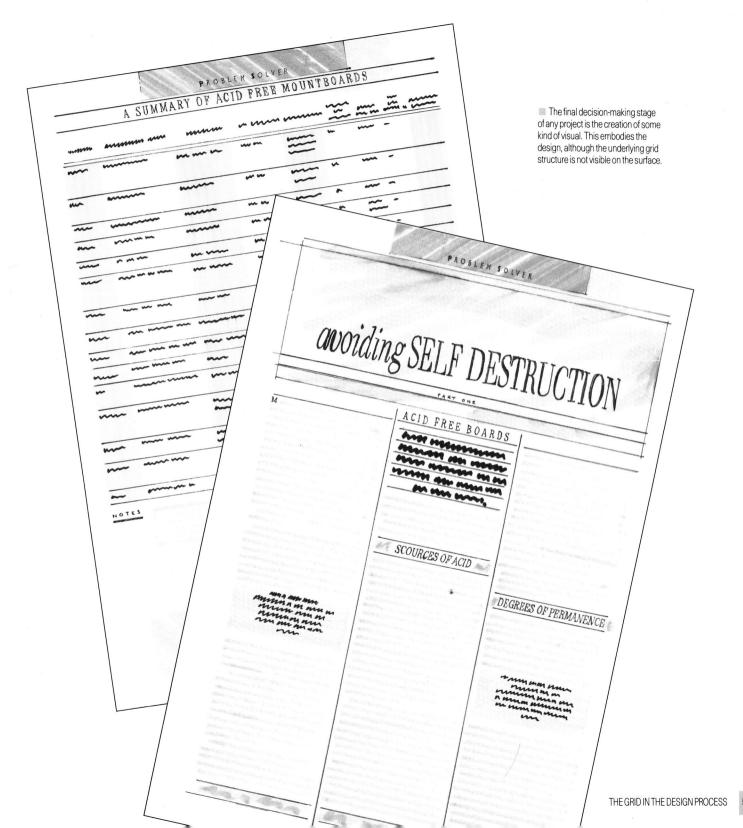

The final decision-making stage of any project is the creation of some kind of visual. This embodies the design, although the underlying grid structure is not visible on the surface.

It is now possible to compare the designer's intention with the appearance of the finished page. The make-up of the page may be slightly adjusted before it goes to print.

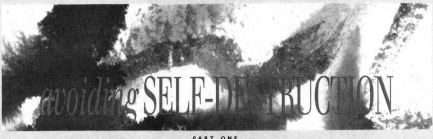

avoiding SELF-DESTRUCTION

PART ONE

ACID FREE BOARDS

MICHELANGELO DELIBERATELY DESTROYED drawings so that only those of a certain standard should survive. All artists are at liberty to do this, but it is another matter if they unwittingly contribute to the destruction of their work. Since the 19th century until very recently, that is exactly what they have been doing by creating works of art on paper that is not acid free. Fortunately this error is widely known now. Yet they persist with an even more absurd activity: paying others to destroy their work. This is what happens when a work on paper is framed to a commercial standard using a mount and backing board that is not acid free.

The papers and boards which existed prior to the 19th century were naturally acid free. This was the result of the simple manufacturing process based on cotton and linen fibres with only pure water and a more or less neutral size being added during production.

If you use the wrong materials to frame your work you could be unknowingly contributing to its rapid decay. ROBERT HAYMAN has been investigating the dangers of acidic attack and how it can be avoided.

matters worse an acid board discolours as it ages and the dyes in facing papers often fade, bringing about a complete change in the appearance of the framed work in addition to the physical damage caused to its substance.

SCOURCES OF ACID

There are three potential sources of acid in wood pulp board. The first is the raw material itself which contains a high proportion of lignin. This is present in all plants and holds them together. It is undesirable since it is very acidic. Cotton fibres are almost pure cellulose with hardly any lignin present, hence their suitability for top quality paper and board. Wood on the other hand contains a mixture of cellulose and lignin so paper and board produced from its untreated pulp are acidic due to the lignin and become yet more acidic as the lignin breaks down. This is most easily illustrated by the ageing of a newspaper which can discolour and become brittle after only a few months. This is what the central core of an ordinary mount board is made of.

The second source of acid are the chemicals used either to break down the wood into pulp or to refine it in order to improve its appearance. For example, it may be bleached to make it whiter. These leave a residue in the pulp unless steps are taken to remove them. Thirdly, acid may be introduced as a component of size, colouring or adhesives used to laminate the board. The most common adulterant of this type is alum which is used as a mordant for dyes and as a precipitant for size based on materials which are not normally compatible with water. In layman's terms the alum is used to 'fix' another component. In both cases this invariably leaves an acidic residue. Solvents, plasticisers and fungicides present in laminating adhesives also pose a potential threat.

One further source of acid remains to be

considered, though this is not directly connected to the board itself. This is atmospheric pollution which may be quite pronounced in towns and cities. This can penetrate into the board and could eventually build up a concentration of acid that becomes harmful. Because of this the latest conservation boards are not only acid free, they are also given an alkaline buffer. This neutralises atmospheric acid and ensures that the board remains acid free for an extensive period of time.

DEGREES OF PERMANENCE

There is more than one way to produce board that is non-acid and therefore there are different types of acid free board. This is potentially misleading as different styles of board result if the raw materials and manufacturing methods are varied. In a few cases

IT SHOULD BE THE MINIUMUM STANDARD FOR ALL MOUNTBOARDS SINCE IT OFFERS A DEGREE OF PROTECTION FOR THE PRESENT AND IMMEDIATE FUTURE.

manufacturers are not as open about this as they should be and the term 'acid free' is used to imply a quality that is not actually on offer. For this reason, artists are obliged to inform themselves about the sub-categories of acid free boards in order to make the most suitable decisions when selecting mounts.

Museum Board or Museum Standard are terms that should be reserved for the very finest quality acid free mount board. This will be 100 per cent cotton and may be constructed as a laminate of papers rather than a pulp core with facing and lining paper. It will be completely acid free and buffered with a small percentage of calcium carbonate (chalk) to protect against atmospheric acid. It will not actually be neutral but should be slightly alkaline with a pH value around 8 or 8.5.

The pH scale is a measure of acidity or alkalinity on which 7 represents neutral. A reading higher than 7 is alkaline whilst below it is acid. Museum quality board will

THIS IS MOST EASILY ILLUSTRATED BY THE AGEING OF A NEWSPAPER WHICH CAN DISCOLOUR AND BECOME BRITTLE AFTER ONLY A FEW MONTHS.

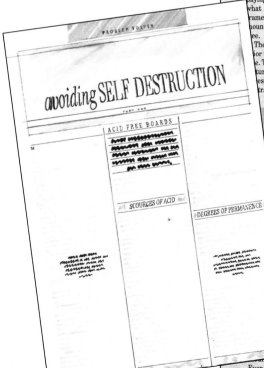

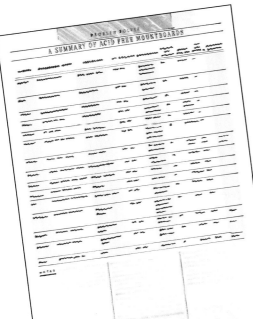

Technical information can be displayed attractively by the carefully considered use of colour, rules and the typeface. Whatever the project, it should always reflect the quality and image of the medium for which it is designed.

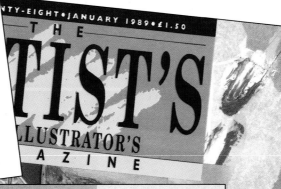

CHECKLIST

- Discuss the requirements for the design with your client.
- Agree on a size for the design.
- Decide on a shape for the design.
- Work up some thumbnail grid ideas.
- Use these as the basis for your thumbnail sketches.
- Produce as many alternative designs on alternative grids as possible.
- Pay attention to the amount of copy and the space it will occupy; you may need a full-size grid just for this calculation.
- Select the best designs from your thumbnail sketches.
- Work these up to a larger format, paying more attention to the graphic elements.
- Discuss these with your client if necessary.
- Use the intermediate visuals as the basis for further development.
- Plan a finished visual to full size.
- Make sure that your grid can be erased when the elements are in place.
- Remember that your final visual or visuals should represent the final printed form of the design as closely as possible.

P R O B L E M   S O L V E R

A SUMMARY OF ACID FREE MOUNTBOARDS

SUPPLIER	MOUNTBOARD RANGE	DESCRIPTION	pH	BUFFERED	COMPOSITION	NUMBER OF COLOURS	SHEET SIZE INS	RRP PER SHEET £	THICKNESS MICRONS
Arquati	Crescent Regular Mat	Acid Free Board	N/S	N/S	Acid free core and backing. Normal surface paper.	141	32×40	—	
Arquati	Crescent Rag Mat	Museum Board	8.2	Yes	100% rag core + acid free surface paper.	63	32×40	—	
Arquati	Crescent Rag Mat '100'	Museum Board	8.2	Yes	100% rag	10	32×40	—	
Arquati	Museum Acid Free	Museum Board	N/S	N/S	N/S	30	32×44/ 31½×39½	—	
Arquati	HT Acid Free	Acid Free Board	N/S	N/S	N/S	15	32×39½	—	
Atlantis	Canson Fine Art Boards	Acid Free Board	N/S	N/S	Acid free core and backing with quality drawing paper facing	50	80×120cm	6.50	
Atlantis	Atlantis 100% Cotton	Museum Board	8.5	Yes	100% Cotton	3	33×45 33×47	8.50 8.66	1,650 1,650
Atlantis	Atlantis Conservation Board	Conservation Board	8.5	Yes	Refined alpha-cellulose pulp	2	33×47	5.38	
Atlantis	Atlantis Neutral Mount Board	Neutral Board	N/S	Yes	Neutralised pulp	23	32×44	2.47	
Daler-Rowney	Studland Museum Board	Museum Board	N/S	Yes	100% Cotton	3	46½×33¾	13.10	
Daler-Rowney	Studland Conservation Board	Acid Free Conservation Board	8.5	Yes	Refined Cellulose Pulp	26	32×44	3.65	
Nielsen	Bainbridge Mountboard	Acid Free Board	N/S	Yes	Acid free core and backing paper. Surface paper N/S.	99	40×60	1.78	
Nielsen	Bainbridge Alphamount	Archival Board	8.3	Yes	Bleached cellulose pulp	2	40×60	3.39	975

INTRODUCTION

THE GRAPHIC DESIGN INDUSTRY is divided into different areas, which traditionally tend to specialize in their own chosen form of graphic communication. Even the methods of working within these areas vary. For instance, the world of advertising separates the creative jobs into different patterns from those found in general design consultancy. The publishing industry tackles the creative process in yet another way. The only factor that these industries have in common is that the work they produce must be visually effective and dynamically creative.

However, no matter what area of the industry you work in, you will have one attribute. Whether you are an advertising agency art director, a specialist graphic designer or an art editor/designer, you must understand and be able to apply the rules of composition to your design work.

The major compositional feature that both underlies and influences the design work that surrounds us is the expressive and creative work that is achieved with the aid of a grid. All designers need to know how to work using a structured formula.

A designer with many years of experience will tend to divide space visually, without appearing to use an obvious structure. Even when the designer is questioned about this, it is possible that he will be unaware of the knowledge he has and will be unable to explain how the design evolved. This is simply because the knowledge has become second nature in the design process. Like the musician who does not need to refer to scales, the experienced designer may make no obvious reference to grids. He may often forget or put behind him the formal training he received when studying his subject. Once a designer has become a confident and competent professional, it is possible for him to relate to the design space in a more abstract way. He will know the right and wrong ways in which the design elements can be applied. He will identify type styles at given proportions and instinctively know the sizes and positions that would suit these best. He will use pictorial material to create stress and to counterbalance the other graphic elements. This will be done visually and often without reference to measurement. In fact, once you are able to break away from formal grids, new and original design concepts can often be achieved. However, I do not believe that it is possible to use space effectively without some grounding in composition.

GRIDS AND THE DESIGN INDUSTRY

As I mentioned earlier, the different areas of graphic design and the professionals within these areas approach their work with a different emphasis. An advertising art director will often scribble down the concept, totally disregarding the design as it will eventually appear. His only interest is in producing an effective piece of communication. The task of piecing the design and its composition together will be left to the visualizer, an expert at composing elements and giving them the right weight and emphasis in a balanced and harmonious composition. As you consider the work on the following pages, look out for the compositional tricks applied by these professionals. You will be able to study the variety of compositional grid arrangements arrived at by the designer working in general design consultancies, and you will also see the variation of mood and theme in the work of designers operating in the publishing industry. Books and magazines are obvious areas to discover grids, but you should be conscious, when studying this work, of the subtle nuances that have been evolved over the years.

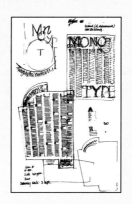

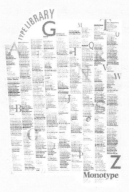

■ Innovators in the use of grids in design, such as David Quay, whose work is shown here, prove that there are no limits to the creative exploitation of grids.

Grids in design and print

SOME PROJECTS begin when the designer creates the grid, which will be his personal choice and the inspirational source for his design. On the other hand, there are many pieces of design for which the graphics will be developed using an established grid. The differences in this approach to the work depend on the particular areas of graphics in which you are working. If, for instance, you were working on an established magazine, it is almost certain that the grid formula will already have been decided. If, however, the work is beginning from scratch – for a one-off brochure, poster or package, for example – the compositional grid will be designed in the initial stages of the project.

To discover the underlying composition of any piece of printed work you must uncover its essential compositional feature – the grid. On these pages you will see a number of designs in their finished, printed state. To help reveal the compositional secrets, I have overlaid the base grids that were the initial formulae used by the designers in the creative decision-making process. It will help you further to understand this work if you select some printed specimens for yourself and work out their roots.

You will be surprised that what superficially appears to be a simple design formula emerges out of a quite complex base. The reverse situation, when complex formulae are derived from simple bases, will also become evident. I stress this to make you aware that finished designs cannot be dismissed as being obvious. A complex process of design, consultation and decision making lies beneath all the finished print that surrounds us.

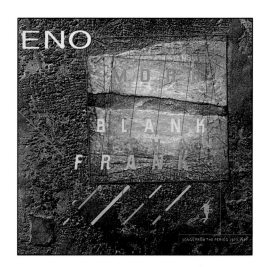

This modern record sleeve makes clear use of the grid by incorporating it as a printed visual device to enhance the decorative quality of the surface.

■ What appears to be a simple
design has, in fact, a complex
compositional structure. The grid
has been offset to allow white space
at the extreme left and base, while
the design is hinged from the left-
hand edge of the main illustration.

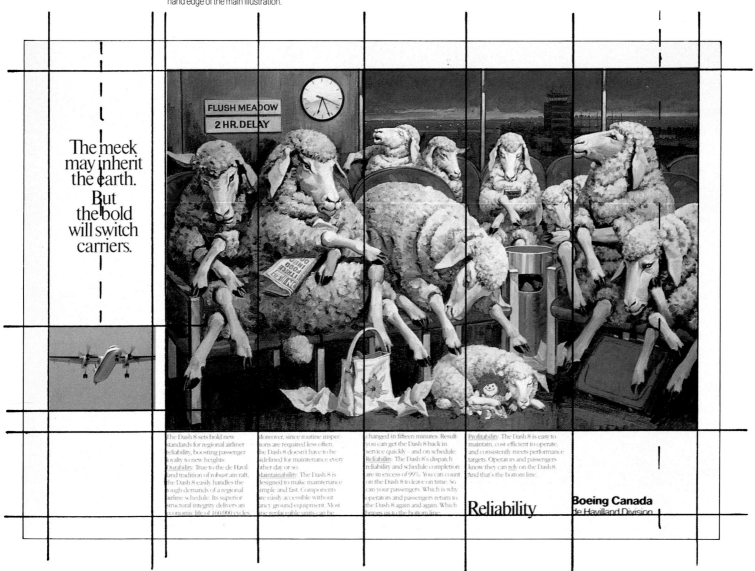

The meek
may inherit
the earth.
But
the bold
will switch
carriers.

FLUSH MEADOW
2 HR. DELAY

The Dash 8 sets bold new
standards for regional airliner
reliability, boosting passenger
loyalty to new heights.
Durability. True to the de Havilland tradition of robust aircraft,
the Dash 8 easily handles the
tough demands of a regional
airline schedule. Its superior
structural integrity delivers an
economic life of 160,000 cycles.

Moreover, since routine inspec-
tions are required less often,
the Dash 8 doesn't have to be
sidelined for maintenance every
other day or so.
Maintainability. The Dash 8 is
designed to make maintenance
simple and fast. Components
are easily accessible without
fancy ground equipment. Most
line replaceable units can be

changed in fifteen minutes. Result:
you can get the Dash 8 back in
service quickly – and on schedule.
Reliability. The Dash 8's dispatch
reliability and schedule completion
are in excess of 99%. You can count
on the Dash 8 to leave on time. So
can your passengers. Which is why
operators and passengers return to
the Dash 8 again and again. Which
brings us to the bottom line.

Profitability. The Dash 8 is easy to
maintain, cost efficient to operate,
and consistently meets performance
targets. Operators and passengers
know they can rely on the Dash 8.
And that's the bottom line.

Reliability

Boeing Canada
de Havilland Division

The formula behind the design

TO DEMYSTIFY THE design process and to see how ideas evolve in the design industry you need to have access to the methods adopted by individual designers. Having access to the designer's thoughts and seeing these presented in rough form is, perhaps, the best way of discovering the practicalities that underlie, and creativity that goes into, a piece of work. Your creative powers will be enhanced by carefully studying the top designers and their working methods. I have selected a number of appropriate visual stages from a series of original design projects to depict the compositional devices in a variety of different ways. To illustrate this further, I have included the printed work to show how the final piece has emerged. I am sure that from these you will gain a fuller realization of the evolutionary stages in the design industry.

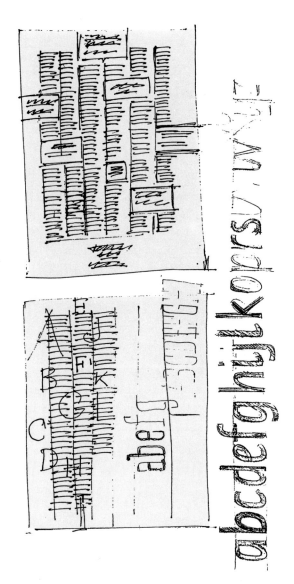

■ The brief to designer David Quay was to create an innovative and modern wallchart showing typefaces. The first visuals hint at a traditional and conventional formula.

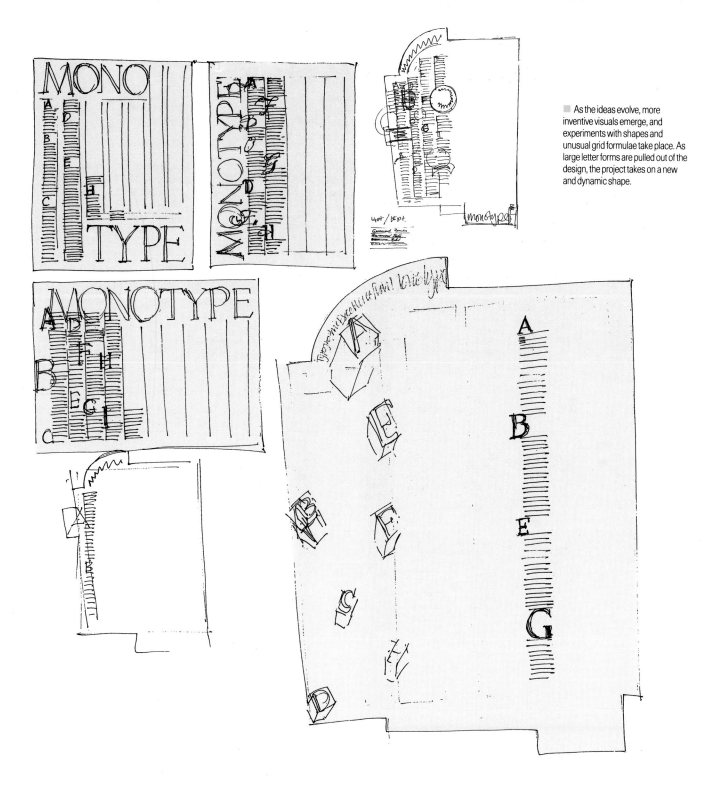

As the ideas evolve, more inventive visuals emerge, and experiments with shapes and unusual grid formulae take place. As large letter forms are pulled out of the design, the project takes on a new and dynamic shape.

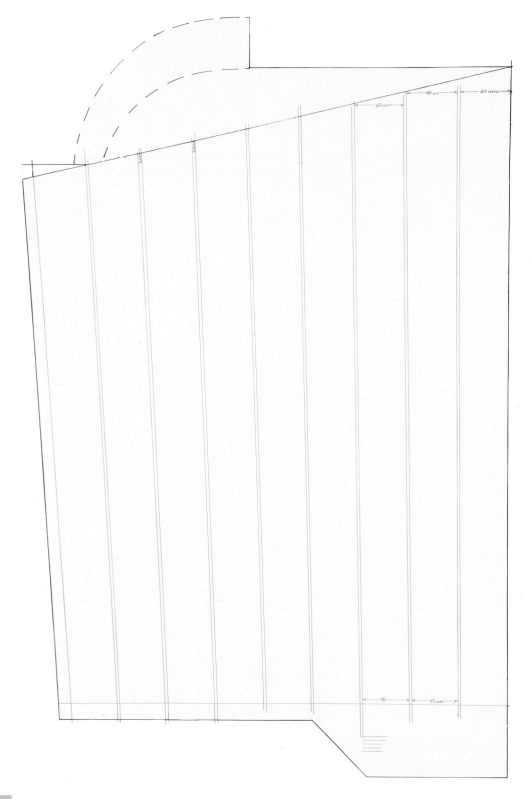

The actual grid used in the design for the Monotype wallchart is shown here. You will notice that, although the columns are carefully measured, they do not have consistent widths throughout, and it is this that makes the design unique.

The scamp for the final design loosely arranges the elements in almost perfect proportion to echo the finished print.

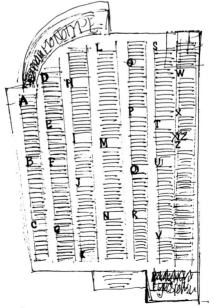

TYPE LIBRARY

Monotype

The final printed wallchart confirms the experimental possibilities of combining today's technology with the inventive use of an unusual grid, to create interesting and varied design shapes and to ensure the visual balance of the image.

Advertising

THE KEY TO ADVERTISING layout and design is the influence of a current mode or trend. Advertising design appears to go through fashions. The designs are heavily influenced by a number of highly creative and forward-moving design agencies, which are renowned for setting styles of advertising communication. The massive competition that challenges every printed advertisement you see makes it the task of the specialist to arrive at stylish and appropriate designs that rely, as any design does, on good compositional invention. These designs are, therefore, good subjects for investigation as some have been cleverly invented. You will see a number of advertising layouts, and study them from their raw, initial state as mere concepts and embryos of design ideas, through to the subtle fine-tuning that finishes in print. You will also recognize how grids have been designed to accommodate these ideas, and through this you will realize that the advertising designer uses the grid as a mere scaffold on which the idea is elaborated.

Advertising design divides into many areas. The main source of design work revolves around printed advertisements, for which much of the design imagery is dynamic and forceful. The method of working is innovative, yet it sometimes lacks subtlety. You must have seen some of the national advertising in which electrical goods, for example, are listed and illustrated in columns. Bursting through this regimentation will be an illustration or some bold type emphasizing a particular feature, a new spectacular technical development or even a special price offer. These advertisements, and the thousands that have been produced in this vein, require all the designer's skill and ingenuity to give a new visual twist to a familiar sales story. The designers who produce these images are creative and highly skilled in this particular area. Study these advertisements closely and compare the ways in which the grids have been manipulated. There is a great deal to be learned from such a simple source.

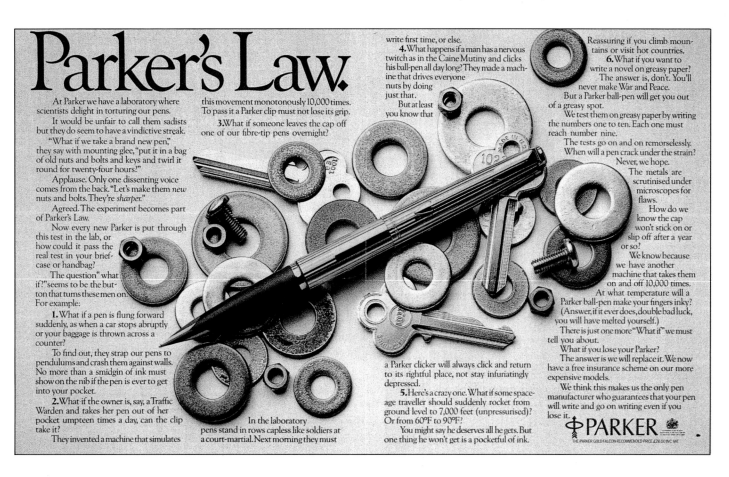

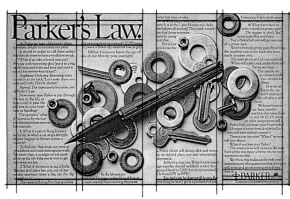

■ This advertisement relies on a simple two-column grid on each page. The central gutter is slightly wider than the outer margins to allow for the binding, but the pages are united by the central dynamic illustration, which appears to be placed at random but is, in fact, cleverly positioned.

On the diagram you can see the cunning structure of the grid formula, sandwiched between the main heading and the sign-off logo at the end of the text.

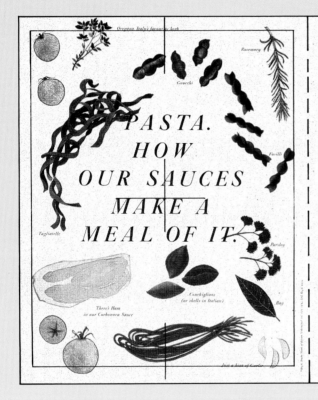

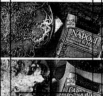

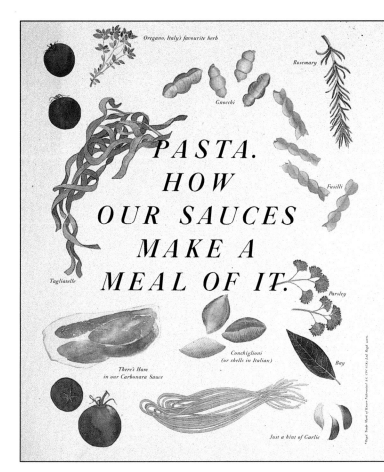

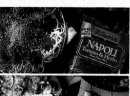

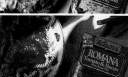

The advertisement shown here uses a magazine style of grid formula to persuade the reader that they are reading an editorial article. The left-hand pictorial grid is a marginal structure for the positioning of visual elements and centred text. The right-hand page uses a traditional three-column grid, heavy with text, with a central, compelling arrangement of photographs that directly links to the facing page. To finish this design, the logo is picked out in colour so that it punctuates the bottom of the page and finishes the story.

Poster design

NOT EVERY POSTER requires an obvious grid structure, of course, although I feel that in order to divide any design space you have to calculate and create proportional measurements. The compositional feel projected by the design elements must be harmoniously balanced to express both the content and the quality and style that is appropriate to the concept. If there are just a few words as the message on your poster, there are innumerable ways in which you can use the space around them, either treating them as a major design feature or reducing them and using the space to communicate the message in another way. An example of a simple solution to the design of a poster with limited text matter is to centre the copy. The grid, or compositional device, in this instance is a central line that divides the area vertically into two equal parts with the graphic elements divided equally across the central measure.

A division can also be created on the horizontal plane. You can divide the visual elements from top to bottom, placing stress in a controlled and measured way. Posters will give you the scope to mix compositional devices with one another. You can centre your main headings while still including a grid layout of, say, two or three columns within the same design space.

Some poster design will carry large photographic or illustrative elements. When deciding which element – the written or the visual – should take visual priority, refer to the original brief or to any research carried out at the beginning of the project. Interesting formulae can be created if text and illustrative images are mixed. Placing a grid over the illustrative area will enable you to ascertain the visual areas that are of the least importance but that are compositionally interesting and in which text can be applied. Photographs can sometimes be used so that they occupy a precise division of a pre-determined grid, leaving space outside the photograph for your text. Posters give you great scope for imaginative and innovative graphic design, and I am sure you can now begin to see that the structure of a poster can be highly refined.

■ The elements for any project are designed individually. The main designs for this poster are shown in rough form as they evolved on the designer's drawing board.

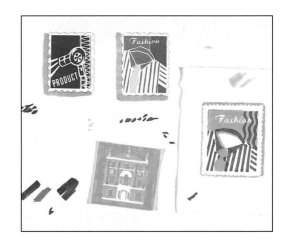

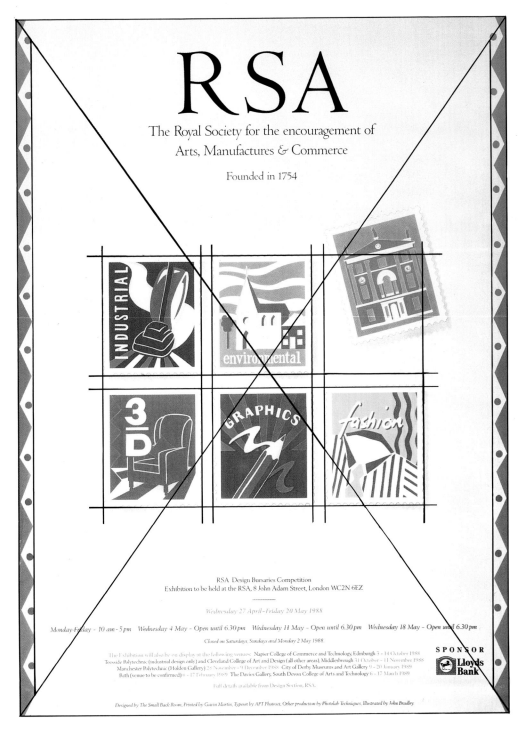

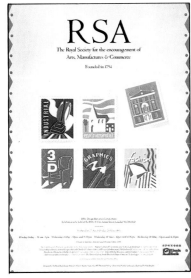

■ This poster incorporates two compositional devices. If you remove the pictorial elements you are left with a centrally divided arrangement of text, with outer margins acting as borders on either side to aid the central focus. Overlaid is a three-column device, which carries the illustrations. The combination of the two would be too tense if it had not been cleverly broken by floating one of the pictorial elements.

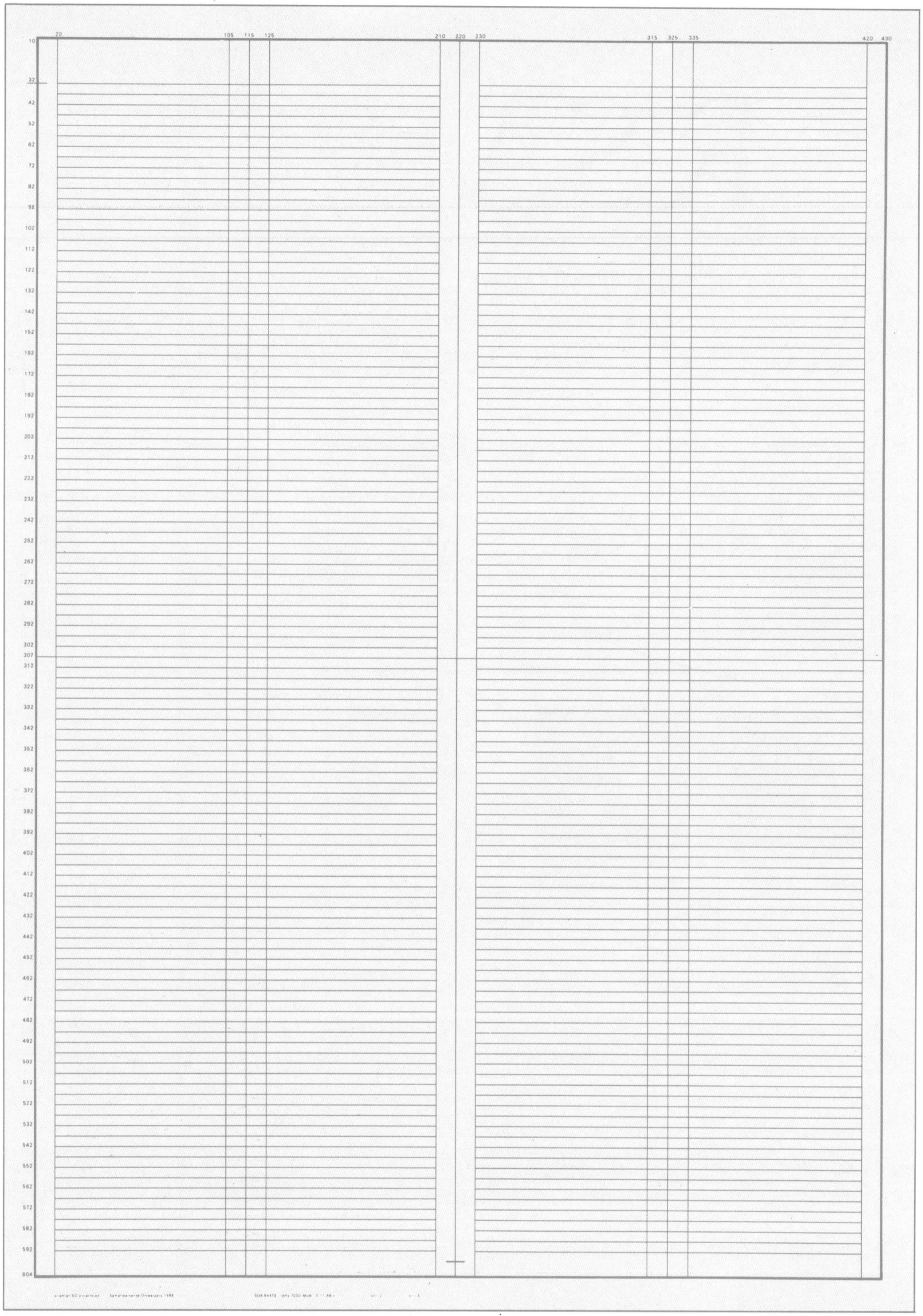
20 105 115 125 210 220 230 315 325 335 420 430
10 32 42 52 62 72 82 92 102 112 122 132 142 152 162 172 182 192 202 212 222 232 242 252 262 272 282 292 302 307 312 322 332 342 352 362 372 382 392 402 412 422 432 442 452 462 472 482 492 502 512 522 532 542 552 567 572 582 592 604

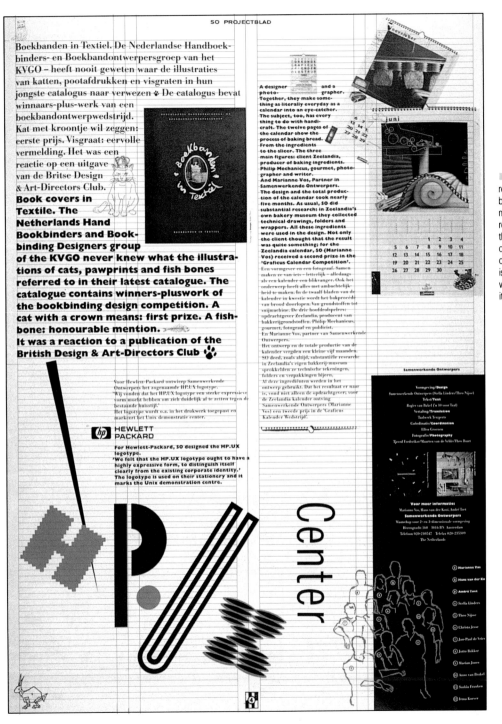

Boekbanden in Textiel. De Nederlandse Handboek-
binders- en Boekbandontwerpersgroep van het
KVGO — heeft nooit geweten waar de illustraties
van katten, pootafdrukken en visgraten in hun
jongste catalogus naar verwezen ❦ De catalogus bevat
winnaars-plus-werk van een
boekbandontwerpwedstrijd.
Kat met kroontje wil zeggen:
eerste prijs. Visgraat: eervolle
vermelding. Het was een
reactie op een uitgave
van de Britse Design
& Art-Directors Club.

**Book covers in
Textile. The
Netherlands Hand
Bookbinders and Book-
binding Designers group
of the KVGO never knew what the illustrations of cats, pawprints and fish bones
referred to in their latest catalogue. The
catalogue contains winners-pluswork of
the bookbinding design competition. A
cat with a crown means: first prize. A fish-
bone: honourable mention.
It was a reaction to a publication of the
British Design & Art-Directors Club**

Voor Hewlett-Packard ontwierp Samenwerkende
Ontwerpers het zogenaamde HP.UX logotype.
"Wij vonden dat het HP.UX logotype een sterke expressieve
vorm moecht hebben om zich duidelijk af te zetten tegen de
bestaande huisstijl.'
Het logotype wordt o.a. in het drukwerk toegepast en
markeert het Unix demonstratie center.

(hp) HEWLETT
PACKARD

For Hewlett-Packard, SO designed the HP.UX
logotype.
'We felt that the HP.UX logotype ought to have a
highly expressive form, to distinguish itself
clearly from the existing corporate identity.'
The logotype is used on their stationery and it
marks the Unix demonstration centre.

A designer   and a
photo-   grapher.
Together, they make some-
thing as literally everyday as a
calendar into an eye-catcher.
The subject, too, has every
thing to do with handi-
craft. The twelve pages of
the calendar show the
process of baking bread.
From the ingredients
to the slicer. The three
main figures: client Zeelandia,
producer of baking ingredients.
Philip Mechanicus, gourmet, photo-
grapher and writer.
And Marianne Vos, Partner in
Samenwerkende Ontwerpers.
The design and the total production of the calendar took nearly
five months. As usual, SO did
substantial research in Zeelandia's
own bakery museum they collected
technical drawings, folders and
wrappers. All these ingredients
were used in the design. Not only
the client thought that the result
was quite something; for the
Zeelandia calendar, SO (Marianne
Vos) received a second prize in the
'Grafiven Calendar Competition'.

Een vormgever en een fotograaf. Samen
maken ze van iets – letterlijk – alledaags
als een kalender een blikvanger. Ook het
onderwerp heeft alles met ambachtelijk-
heid te maken. In de twaalf bladen van de
kalender in kwestie wordt het bakproces
van brood doorlopen. Van grondstoffen tot
snijmachine. De drie hoofdrolspelers:
opdrachtgever Zeelandia, producent van
bakkerijgrondstoffen. Philip Mechanicus,
gourmet, fotograaf en publicist.
En Marianne Vos, partner van Samenwerkende
Ontwerpers.
Het ontwerp en de totale productie van de
kalender vergden een kleine vijf maanden.
SO deed, zoals altijd, substantiële research:
in Zeelandia's eigen bakkerij-museum
sprokkelden ze technische tekeningen,
folders en verpakkingen bijeen.
Al deze ingrediënten werden in het
ontwerp gebruikt. Dat het resultaat er naar
is, vond niet alleen de opdrachtgever; voor
de Zeelandia kalender ontving
Samenwerkende Ontwerpers (Marianne
Vos) een tweede prijs in de 'Grafiven
Kalender Wedstrijd'.

juni

					1	2	3	4
5	6	7	8	9	10	11		
12	13	14	15	16	17	18		
19	20	21	22	23	24	25		
26	27	28	29	30				

Samenwerkende Ontwerpers

Vormgeving/Design
Samenwerkende Ontwerpers (Stella Linders/Theu Nijsse)
Tekst/Text
Roger van Bakel ('t 10 voor Taal)
Vertaling/Translation
Taalwerk Tempets
Coördinatie/Coordination
Ellen Groenen
Fotografie/Photography
Tjeerd Frederikse/Maarten van de Velde/Theu Baart

Voor meer informatie:
Marianne Vos, Hans van der Kooi, André Toet
Samenwerkende Ontwerpers
Maatschap voor 2- en 3-dimensionale vormgeving
Herengracht 160 1016 BN Amsterdam
Telefoon 020-240547 Telefax 020-235509
The Netherlands

① Marianne Vos
② Hans van der Ko
③ André Toet
④ Stella Linders
⑤ Theu Nijsse
⑥ Christa Jesse
⑦ Jan-Paul de Vries
⑧ Jetta Bakker
⑨ Marian Jones
⑩ Anne van Brakel
⑪ Saskia Franken
⑫ Irma Korver

■ This traditional poster, which
reflects much of the discovery made
by the major 20th-century design
movements, uses a detailed,
restrictive underlying grid, in which
the subdivision of space is the result
of an awareness of the arrangement
of compositional balances. The grid
is echoed throughout the design,
without concern or consideration for
its inevitable restrictions.

■ Popular, fun imagery can be created by boldly depicting the main visual elements to give an overall pictorial feel to the design. The grid used in the design of this wallchart has been arranged to follow the visual images. The only constraints imposed on this design are the outer margins, the heading that fits this formula and a centrally positioned visual axis. The text is set in units of one and two columns, but arranged loosely to fit in with the pictures.

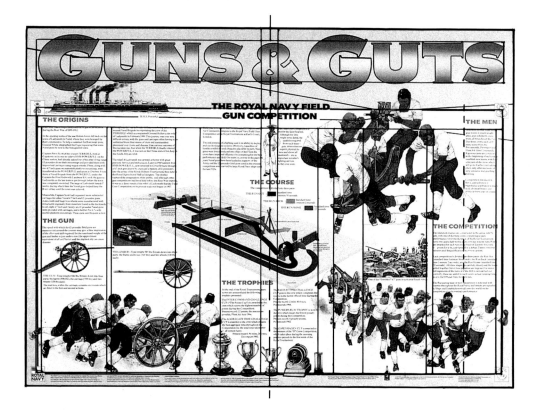

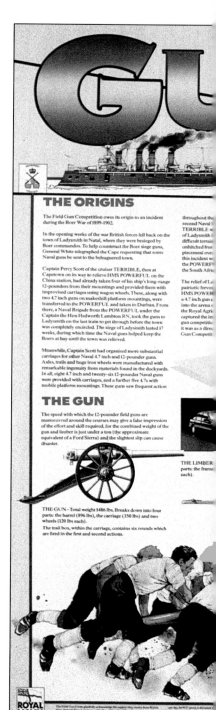

THE ORIGINS

The Field Gun Competition owes its origin to an incident during the Boer War of 1899–1902.

In the opening weeks of the war British forces fell back on the town of Ladysmith in Natal, where they were besieged by Boer commandos. To help counteract the Boer siege guns, General White telegraphed the Cape requesting that some Naval guns be sent to the beleaguered town.

Captain Percy Scott of the cruiser TERRIBLE, then at Capetown on its way to relieve HMS POWERFUL on the China station, had already taken four of his ship's long-range 12-pounders from their mountings and provided them with improvised carriages using wagon wheels. These, along with two 4.7 inch guns on makeshift platform mountings, were transferred to the POWERFUL and taken to Durban. From there, a Naval Brigade from the POWERFUL under the Captain the Hon Hedworth Lambton RN, took the guns to Ladysmith on the last train to get through before the town was completely encircled. The siege of Ladysmith lasted 17 weeks, during which time the Naval guns helped keep the Boers at bay until the town was relieved.

Meanwhile, Captain Scott had organised more substantial carriages for other Naval 4.7 inch and 12-pounder guns. Axles, trails and huge iron wheels were manufactured with remarkable ingenuity from materials found in the dockyards. In all, eight 4.7 inch and twenty-six 12-pounder Naval guns were provided with carriages, and a further five 4.7s with mobile platform mountings. These guns saw frequent action

THE GUN

The speed with which the 12-pounder field guns are manoeuvred around the courses may give a false impression of the effort and skill required, for the combined weight of the gun and limber is just under a ton (the approximate equivalent of a Ford Sierra) and the slightest slip can cause disaster.

THE LIMBER – parts: the frame (each).

THE GUN – Total weight 1486 lbs. Breaks down into four parts: the barrel (896 lbs.), the carriage (350 lbs.) and two wheels (120 lbs each).
The trail box, within the carriage, contains six rounds which are fired in the first and second actions.

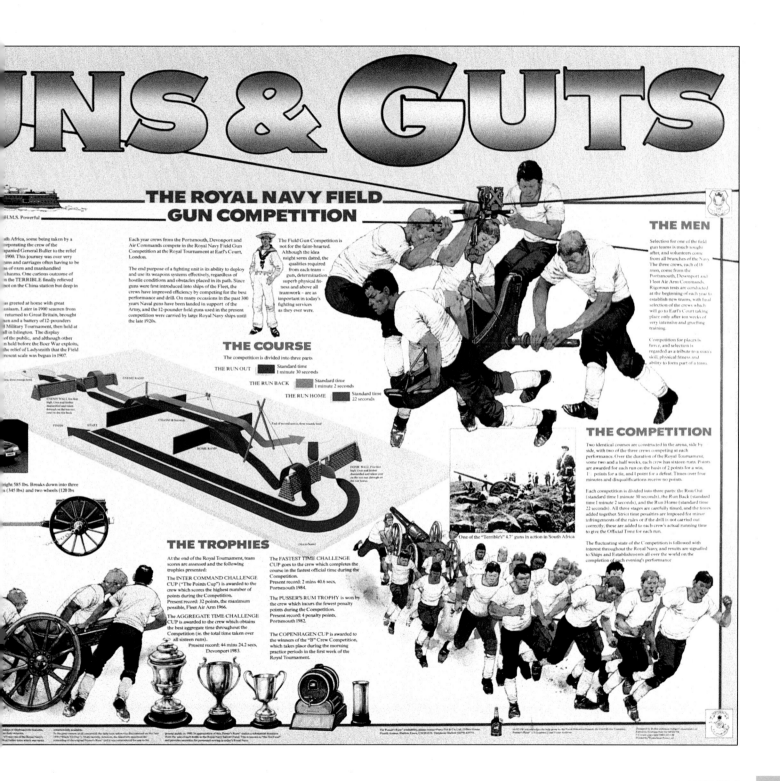

UNS & GUTS

THE ROYAL NAVY FIELD GUN COMPETITION

H.M.S. Powerful

...th Africa, some being taken by a ...orporating the crew of the ...ompanied General Buller to the relief ...1900. This journey was over very ...uns and carriages often having to be ...as of oxen and manhandled ...chasms. One curious outcome of ...n the TERRIBLE finally relieved ...not on the China station but deep in

...as greeted at home with great ...usiasm. Later in 1900 seamen from ...returned to Great Britain, brought ...en and a battery of 12-pounders ...all in Islington. The display ...of the public, and although other ...n held before the Boer War exploits, ...the relief of Ladysmith that the Field ...resent scale was begun in 1907.

Each year crews from the Portsmouth, Devonport and Air Commands compete in the Royal Navy Field Gun Competition at the Royal Tournament at Earl's Court, London.

The end purpose of a fighting unit is its ability to deploy and use its weapons systems effectively, regardless of hostile conditions and obstacles placed in its path. Since guns were first introduced into ships of the Fleet, the crews have improved efficiency by competing for the best performance and drill. On many occasions in the past 300 years Naval guns have been landed in support of the Army, and the 12-pounder field guns used in the present competition were carried by large Royal Navy ships until the late 1920s.

The Field Gun Competition is not for the faint-hearted. Although the idea might seem dated, the qualities required from each team – guts, determination, superb physical fitness and above all teamwork – are as important in today's fighting services as they ever were.

THE MEN

Selection for one of the field gun teams is much sought after, and volunteers come from all branches of the Navy. The three crews, each of 18 men, come from the Portsmouth, Devonport and Fleet Air Arm Commands. Rigorous tests are conducted at the beginning of each year to establish new teams, with final selection of the crews which will go to Earl's Court taking place only after ten weeks of very intensive and gruelling training.

Competition for places is fierce, and selection is regarded as a tribute to a man's skill, physical fitness and ability to form part of a team.

THE COURSE

The competition is divided into three parts.

THE RUN OUT	Standard time 1 minute 30 seconds
THE RUN BACK	Standard time 1 minute 2 seconds
THE RUN HOME	Standard time 22 seconds

ENEMY RAMP

ENEMY WALL, five feet high. Guns and limber disassembled and taken through on the run out, over on the run back.

START

FINISH

CHASM 28 feet wide

HOME RAMP

End of second section, three rounds fired

HOME WALL. Five feet high. Guns and limber reassembled and taken over on the run out, through on the run home.

...ight 585 lbs. Breaks down into three ...s (345 lbs) and two wheels (120 lbs

(Not to Scale)

THE COMPETITION

Two identical courses are constructed in the arena, side by side, with two of the three crews competing at each performance. Over the duration of the Royal Tournament, some two and a half weeks, each crew has sixteen runs. Points are awarded for each run on the basis of 2 points for a win, 1½ points for a tie, and 1 point for a defeat. Times over four minutes and disqualifications receive no points.

Each competition is divided into three parts: the Run Out (standard time 1 minute 30 seconds), the Run Back (standard time 1 minute 2 seconds), and the Run Home (standard time 22 seconds). All three stages are carefully timed, and the times added together. Strict time penalties are imposed for minor infringements of the rules or if the drill is not carried out correctly; these are added to each crew's actual running time to give the Official Time for each run.

The fluctuating state of the Competition is followed with interest throughout the Royal Navy, and results are signalled to Ships and Establishments all over the world on the completion of each evening's performance.

'One of the "Terrible's" 4.7' guns in action in South Africa'

THE TROPHIES

At the end of the Royal Tournament, team scores are assessed and the following trophies presented:

The INTER COMMAND CHALLENGE CUP ("The Points Cup") is awarded to the crew which scores the highest number of points during the Competition.
Present record: 32 points, the maximum possible, Fleet Air Arm 1966.

The AGGREGATE TIME CHALLENGE CUP is awarded to the crew which obtains the best aggregate time throughout the Competition (i.e. the total time taken over all sixteen runs).
Present record: 44 mins 24.2 secs, Devonport 1983.

The FASTEST TIME CHALLENGE CUP goes to the crew which completes the course in the fastest official time during the Competition.
Present record: 2 mins 40.6 secs, Portsmouth 1984.

The PUSSER'S RUM TROPHY is won by the crew which incurs the fewest penalty points during the Competition.
Present record: 4 penalty points, Portsmouth 1982.

The COPENHAGEN CUP is awarded to the winners of the "B" Crew Competition, which takes place during the morning practice periods in the first week of the Royal Tournament.

Leaflets and brochures

THIS AREA OF DESIGN is one in which the grid format as a basis for the design project is absolutely essential. Before you can even begin to consider the design elements in the design space, you will need to invent a grid, and a designer working in this area will probably never omit this stage of the process. Although I am emphasizing the use of a grid, I must point out that the structure of the grid itself will define a lot of the styling and qualities of image that are to emerge. It is important that extensive thought is given to the grid before lengthy and costly visualization begins. You should spend some time researching the designs produced for similar works as a guide to the qualities you are seeking. Take into account the length of copy that is to be included in the project and decide on the priorities you are going to give to the written text. You may decide that the design requires a strong visual appeal, in which case you may produce a design with a large number of columns. This will give you smaller type areas allowing for columns to be left blank and large pictures spanning many columns. Using colour as backgrounds can soften the design area by reducing the stark quality of typesetting, and, by leaving cunning spaces in the colour for illustrations, you can place greater stress on a visual message. Some information will need to be displayed in a more formal manner. In company reports, for example, the words are the important factors, and clear, precise typographic design is essential.

1

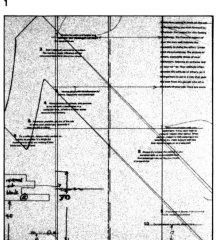

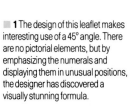 **1** The design of this leaflet makes interesting use of a 45° angle. There are no pictorial elements, but by emphasizing the numerals and displaying them in unusual positions, the designer has discovered a visually stunning formula.

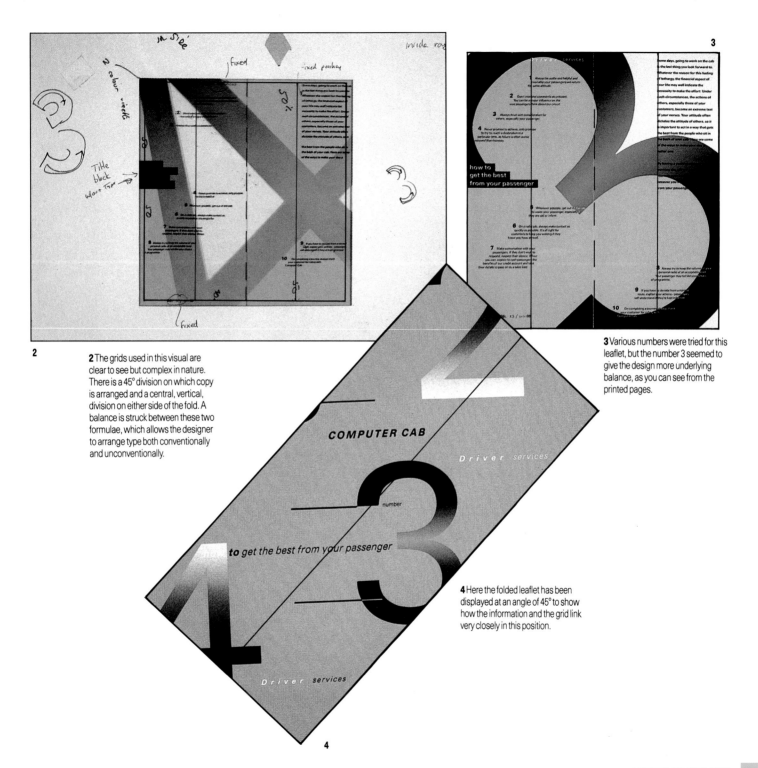

2 The grids used in this visual are clear to see but complex in nature. There is a 45° division on which copy is arranged and a central, vertical, division on either side of the fold. A balance is struck between these two formulae, which allows the designer to arrange type both conventionally and unconventionally.

3 Various numbers were tried for this leaflet, but the number 3 seemed to give the design more underlying balance, as you can see from the printed pages.

4 Here the folded leaflet has been displayed at an angle of 45° to show how the information and the grid link very closely in this position.

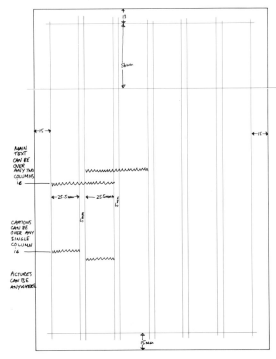

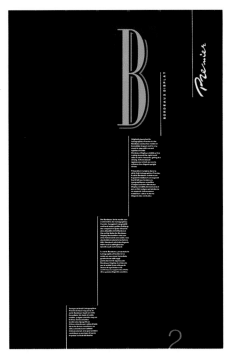

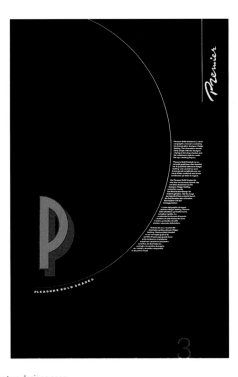

■ **Above left** The designs here use a six-column grid. The flexibility this offers in spatial terms gives the designer an abundance of opportunities to develop creative formulae.

■ **Above** The two designs seen above, while totally different in concept are linked by the underlying grid structure. Their proportions are equally balanced, giving the appearance of the same character performing a different trick.

An abundance of brochures is produced every year, especially in the travel industry, where brochures compete for customers' attention. Study the styles adopted by the travel industry, and see how often the art of the travel brochure lies in its ability to communicate a price image from the moment it is picked from the shelf. These brochures must sell their services instantly, and the designs produced for these companies are almost scientifically controlled.

One area in which you will have more creative control is the production of the corporate image brochure. The companies commissioning this work are concerned to look more modern and stylish than their nearest competitor.

Grids used in the styling and creation of leaflets and brochures should be viewed as a flexible creative tool that will help you to solve a major part of the design problem.

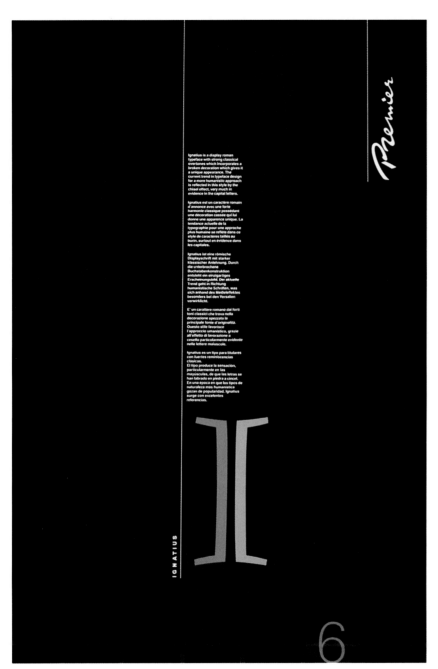

IGNATIUS

Premier

Ignatius is a display roman typeface with strong classical overtones which incorporates a broken decoration which gives it a unique appearance. The current trend in typeface design for a more humanistic approach is reflected in this style by the chisel effect, very much in evidence in the capital letters.

Ignatius est un caractère romain d'annonce avec une forte harmonie classique possédant une decoration cassée qui lui donne une apparence unique. La tendance actuelle de la typographie pour une approche plus humaine se reflète dans ce style de caractères taillés au burin, surtout en évidence dans les capitales.

Ignatius ist eine römische Displayschrift mit starker klassischer Anlehnung. Durch die unterbrochene Buchstabenkonstruktion entsteht ein einzigartiges Erscheinungsbild. Der aktuelle Trend geht in Richtung humanistische Schriften, was sich anhand des Meißeleffektes besonders bei den Versalien verwirklicht.

È un carattere romano dai forti toni classici che trova nella decorazione spezzata in principale fonte di originalità. Questo stile favorisce l'approccio umanistico, grazie all'effetto di lavorazione a cesello particolarmente evidente nelle lettere maiuscole.

Ignatius es un tipo para titulares con fuertes reminiscencias clásicas. El tipo produce la sensación, particularmente en las mayúsculas, de que las letras se han labrado en piedra a cincel. En una epoca en que los tipos de naturaleza mas humanistica gozan de popularidad, Ignatius surge con excelentes referencias.

6

◼ **Left** This more formal central arrangement is counter-balanced by the positioning of almost mechanical design devices. The space engulfs you visually, yet the presence and position of the devices allow the eye to escape.

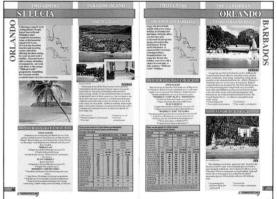

◼ **Above** This typical holiday brochure relies heavily on design devices. The formal arrangement of columns is broken up with bands of colour, in which type is reversed out. Text is run vertically in the margins, and the occasional tint and hint of colour are carefully positioned within the grid.

Packaging

GRIDS ARE NOT COMMONLY associated with packaging, although, like most pieces of design, the surfaces of a three-dimensional package are simply design areas that demand the same compositional consideration as any two-dimensional design space. Most packages will carry two distinct elements of design. The first of these could be a graphic device or creatively controlled typographic imagery that has the freedom to span the surface of the pack in whatever way is appropriate or effective. The second part of the design, which will be just as important to the overall concept or image but which may occupy a more restrained and restrictive place within the design, is the descriptive typography and information that your pack will be obliged to display. A formula for linking these two components in harmonious balance is vital.

Remember that, because your pack is three-dimensional, the grid does not necessarily have to run in a conventional straight line. In fact, techniques like the spiralling of a grid around the pack will help you to present information in a flowing, visual way. Although your pack will contain its individual planes, try to use its three dimensions in an imaginative and creative manner.

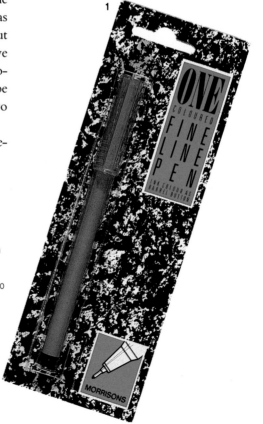

1 The grid used for this bubble pack is so arranged that the item on sale can be displayed without interference from any information, although the product is positioned to complement the grid formula.

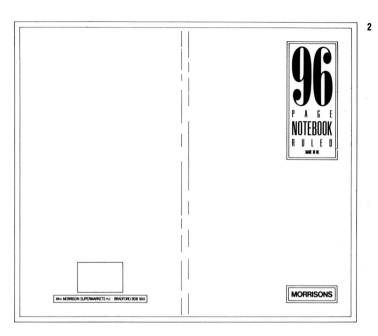

2

2 & 3 These two examples of packaging artwork show how the single-column grid has been positioned in a way that invites the left-hand space to be filled with a picture or the actual product.

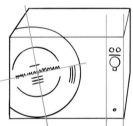

4 These packages for light bulbs use a similar formula to the other designs shown on this page. The product itself is printed in the space, with information centrally displayed, but at an angle to separate it visually from the information on the pack.

3

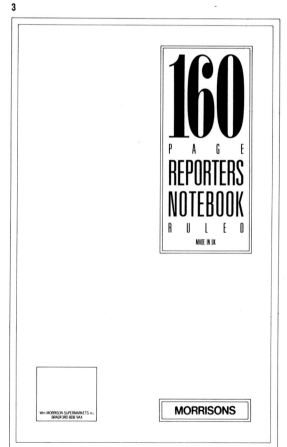

4

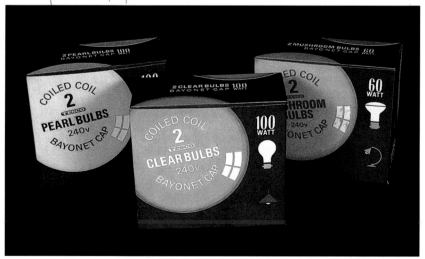

Newsletters and newspapers

WHEN YOU ARE DESIGNING for a company newsletter it is essential that you create a sensible yet flexible grid. In the initial stages the newsletter will probably be produced from a limited amount of information, which will tend to be generated by the employees of the company. The authors will expect this to be communicated in an effective but interesting manner. This newsletter performs two functions. Its first job is to update and inform a target readership, and if it is to perform this function effectively, the visual presentation is paramount to its success. The second objective is to maintain this flow of information on a regular basis. In order to retain a sense of continuity and to establish a corporate image, it is essential that the choices you made at the beginning of the project are appropriate for subsequent issues.

The choice of grid should be carefully considered as it will form a structure for all the text that will be set from this point on. If you choose to start with a three-column grid, the text will always be set to this specification. This convention is adopted for the sake of overall consistency. It allows you to make one calculation for the text that is submitted and permits easier layout design when the newsletter is being put together.

To make your newsletter distinctive, however, some creative innovations are necessary. Given the economics of printing, it is likely that you will be restricted to one colour or perhaps a maximum of two colours. If you include the tints from these colours you can create some interesting visual devices. Photographs can be printed with the second colour to create duotones. Headings and sub-headings can be set in different typefaces. Large capital letters can be dropped in at the beginning of a sentence or paragraph. All these devices will act as visual patterns to help break up the columns of type. The use of white space will be restricted in this type of work, so it is important that you make the most of the graphic elements that you can use. Remember, however, that whatever you do must be suitable for the months and years to come.

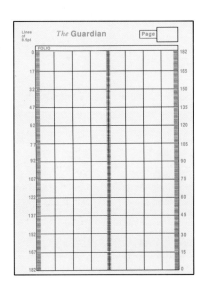

■ The master grid needs to be well thought out and structured to allow the user quickly and easily to measure the design space. As the column widths are set to regular, established sizes, it is possible to divide the page both vertically and horizontally. Desk-top publishing uses grids of this type for easy design manoeuvrability.

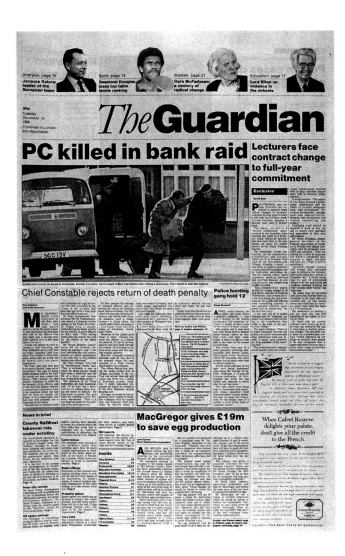

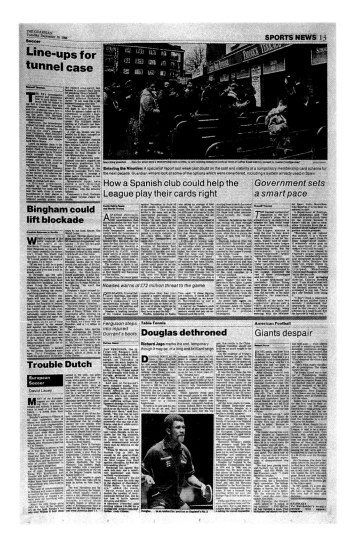

Newspapers tend to keep rigidly to an established grid, and it is only when a brand new publication appears that the choice of grid is left to the designer. All newspapers follow a house style, and even the type styles and their proportions are fairly rigidly governed. The principal duty of designers involved in newspaper layout is to maintain the newspaper's established image, although occasionally a news-paper will undertake a programme of deliberate and well-researched re-design. In general, though, the newspaper designer has to use his verve and creativity to ensure a lively and captivating page design within the constraints of the house style.

Both newsletters and newspapers rely on the subtle manipulation of typographic images and graphic devices within a regular and systematic grid.

■ This newspaper design demonstrates how a mass of information can be displayed in a subtle and meaningful way while still allowing great variety in presentation. The appropriate inclusion of a line or tint ribbon or a change in setting allows different patterns to be enjoyed.

Magazines

MAGAZINES, LIKE THE NEWSPAPERS, rely on an established grid, although the use of more than one grid format within a single magazine is not uncommon; indeed, it is a design feature that is exploited to give visual variety to the pages of editorial matter. The appearance of these established pages is often pre-determined by the grid format, which has been distinguished from the grid used for the rest of the matter to alter the look of the magazine at a given point. The grid design is paramount in the styling of a magazine as not only will it affect the overall appearance but it will set its tone in the market place. You have probably noticed recently that the more up-market magazines have placed more importance on the individual design of each of the feature articles than do their less stylish counterparts. These up-market magazines expect the designer to reflect a feeling of the content of each individual article, which is likely to be supported by illustrative or photographic matter. The type styles and their proportions are often enhanced by the use of white space to surround them.

The design of established, leading magazines is cultivated to retain the qualities that their public has grown to expect, and, in my opinion, the styling sometimes takes priority over the content.

■ The front covers of most magazines have established design features such as the masthead. These elements have a predetermined position and size, leaving the remaining space for other design features, which will vary from issue to issue. This means that the pre-set format or grid of the front cover imposes restrictions on the emerging design. Below is a dummy layout for a cover showing the possible position of headings and drop-in images.

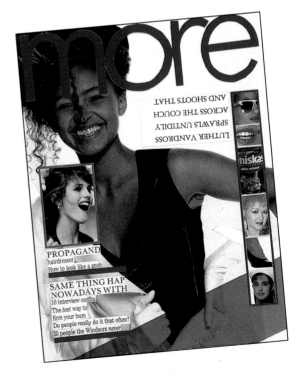

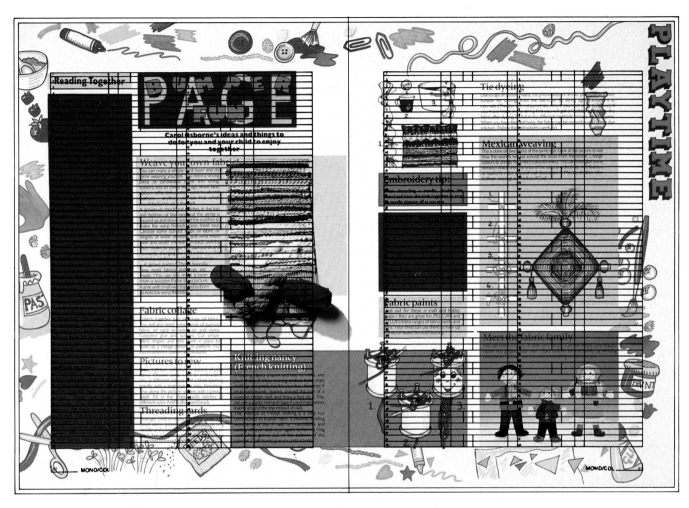

Once a grid is established and the designer is experienced and familiar with the format, it is possible to create vivid and lively layouts, as you can see from the full-colour, double-page spread shown here.

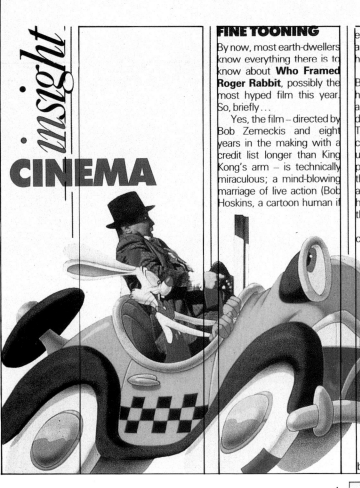

insight
CINEMA

FINE TOONING

By now, most earth-dwellers know everything there is to know about **Who Framed Roger Rabbit**, possibly the most hyped film this year. So, briefly…

Yes, the film – directed by Bob Zemeckis and eight years in the making with a credit list longer than King Kong's arm – is technically miraculous; a mind-blowing marriage of live action (Bob Hoskins, a cartoon human if ever there was one) and animation (Roger Rabbit and his sultry wife Jessica).

Yes, the story – in which Bob Hoskins' sorry gumshoe helps cartoon star Roger beat a false murder rap – is a wonderfully clever spoof of 40s Tinseltown. The studio cattle calls are attended, quite naturally, by cattle and, more pointedly, the Toons live in their own segregated town and perform strictly for humans in a club not unlike the Cotton Club.

And yes, *Roger Rabbit* is certain to be the numero uno Christmas movie. Just one snag – Roger. Far from being a lovable bunny (like Bugs who, with Daffy and Donald, has a walk-on part), Roger's a prime candidate for the 'dip' – an evil solvent concocted by the no-good Judge Doom (Christopher Lloyd) and the only way to shut-up an irksome Toon. High on decibels, low on sou but ideal for unruly nephews

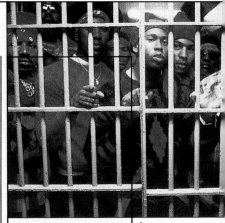

NOW SHOWING
● **COLORS**
Hopper's controversial and gut-crunching gang wars flick (above) pairing Sean Penn and Robert Duvall as an odd couple of LA cops.
● **TUCKER**
One man and his car; Coppola's mythic ode to maverick auto ace, played – lovingly – by Jeff Bridges.
● **THE DAWNING**
Very delicate, very tasteful and utterly British period drama about a young Irish girl's political awakening. With Anthony Hopkins, Jean Simmons and the last of Trevor Howard.

ELISSA VAN POZNAK

1

1 Magazines carry different styles and images. You can see from the visual for this double-page spread that the emphasis is on vertical and horizontal blocks. This layout gives a solid and structured look, which differs greatly from the page from *Elle* seen above.

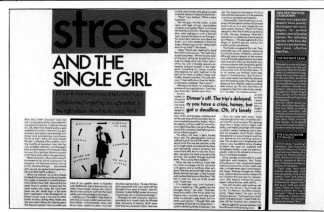

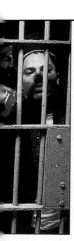

TAXING LYRICAL

Only Juzo Itami, the creator of last year's extraordinary *Tampopo*, would think of making a female tax inspector the heroine of his new film, *A Taxing Woman*.

Itami's wife, Nobuko Miyamoto (below), so captivating in *Tampopo*, plays a divorced single parent whose job – investigating a ruthless but irresistible wheeler-dealer named Gondo – becomes an obsession.

Itami's latest is a sexy, seductively crafted send-up which says more about Japan and modern Japanese women (our heroine stakes out tax-dodgers from behind a copy of Japanese ELLE) than any documentary.

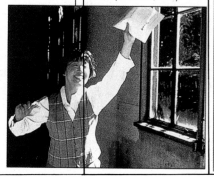

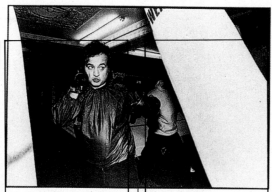

Punch drunk: the Belushi tragedy hits the screen

RUSHES

● **The horror, the horror: not only is *Nightmare on Elm Street 4* outgrossing (sic) its predecessors, but Freddy (Robert Englund) will star in his own TV series... Unknown chubby Michael Chiklis plays tragic John Belushi in biopic *Wired*. Robert De Niro and Robin Williams will *not* play themselves ... Jamaica's buzzing with a remake of the classic *Lord of the Flies*. Rising Harry Hook (*The Kitchen Toto*) directs... Marlon Brando is alive and well having just completed anti-apartheid drama *A Dry White Season*.**

BLUE BIRD

Clint Eastwood's **Bird** – which dramatises the final act in the life of jazz genius Charlie Parker (who died in 1955, aged 34) – is a sombre and sobering film, as dark in tone as it is to look at.

Yet, for all its eerie authenticity – Eastwood brilliantly recreates Parker's nocturnal world and uses an original Bird soundtrack – *Bird* is ultimately a celebration; a tribute. Forest Whitaker is tremendously moving as the articulate, capricious bear of a man racked with pain (much of it self-induced) and tormented by the impossible paradox of being an artist, a family man and a junkie.

Fortunately, some sparkling humour leavens the tragedy (and some slightly suspect cymbal-ism) – as when Parker and band, down on their luck, play a Jewish wedding, or when Bird serenades his bird on horseback. As Chan, Parker's spirited wife, Diane Venora is also splendid. So is Samuel E Wright's uncanny portrayal of Dizzy Gillespie.

But it is Whitaker who really makes *Bird* fly.

Blue notes from the Birdman of jazz

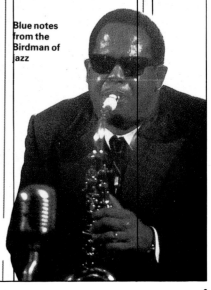

2 The design of magazine pages is often influenced by external factors. The bottom half of this double-page spread has been allocated to advertising, and the designer has been obliged to create a layout that works within the remaining shape.

Books

THE DESIGNS USED in book publishing vary from the simplest of formats to the most complex, flexible and interchangeable of grids. The majority of books published fall into the category that I will define as the single-column grid format. Although this design is fairly predictable, you will remember that a number of alternative page designs can be explored. Comparing two apparently similar published works will show you that there are differences, and that even on this scale, great creative control is possible.

In the broader aspects of the book publishing industry there are limitless opportunities to exploit the exciting and imaginative creativity that can be evolved from any given project. In the glossier world of publishing, grids and the designs they embody are extremely important, giving an authoritative image while at the same time conveying the information through text and illustrative matter in a highly practical manner.

If a series of books is to be created, it is usual to establish a format that is comfortable to handle, yet able to accommodate unforeseen future developments. For this book, which is one of a family of books, a grid format was developed. The column measure is consistent throughout the series, and even the space around the written and visual matter is pre-determined. The designs of books are so numerous that a careful study of this area of work can be carried out only by extensive research into what is currently being produced.

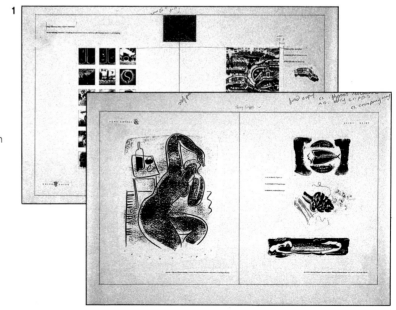

1 These photocopies of page layouts for a company book show an easy method of working in which the visual imagery can be reproduced in rough form and pasted into position on the grid format.

3

How to Airbrush.....

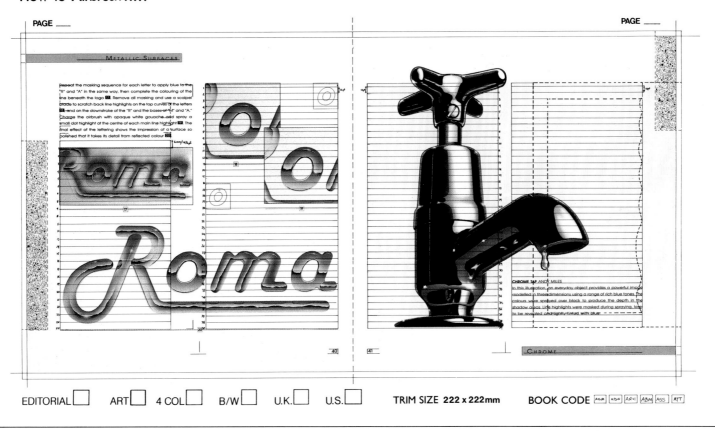

PAGE ____

PAGE ____

METALLIC SURFACES

Repeat the masking sequence for each letter to apply blue to the "R" and "A" in the same way, then complete the colouring of the line beneath the logo 16. Remove all masking and use a scalpel blade to scratch back line highlights on the top curves of the letters 18, and on the downstroke of the "R" and the base of "M" and "A". Charge the airbrush with opaque white gouache, add spray a small dot highlight at the centre of each main line highlight 17. The final effect of the lettering shows the impression of a surface so polished that it takes its detail from reflected colour 20.

CHROME TAP ANDY MILES
In this illustration, an everyday object provides a powerful image modelled in three dimensions using a range of rich blue tones. The colours were sprayed over black to produce the depth in the shadow areas. Line highlights were masked during spraying, later to be revealed and lightly-tinted with blue.

CHROME

EDITORIAL ☐ ART ☐ 4 COL ☐ B/W ☐ U.K. ☐ U.S. ☐ **TRIM SIZE 222 x 222mm** **BOOK CODE** AGM AGG ARH ABM ASS ATT

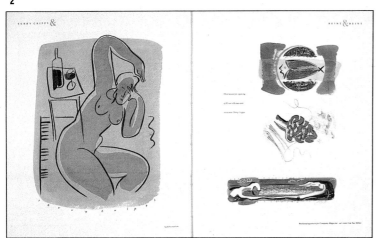

2 The finished book, for which the layouts in **1** were produced, uses the space in an apparently random fashion, although further pages show that the position of each of the elements has a precise relationship to the others. This is achieved through using the same grid for each page.

3 The grid for this book on airbrush techniques has established features that are located on the grid and appear on every page. The grid provides a formalized guide for the typesetting, graphic devices and the columns, which can be merged into central blocks.

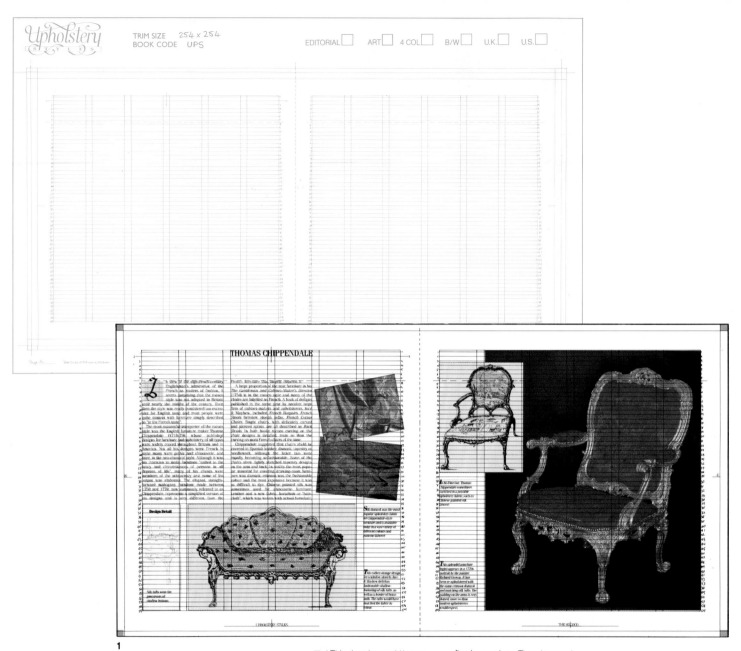

1 This six-column grid layout gives enormous flexibility to the designer. The setting is placed over two of the columns, leaving interesting spaces for pictures and floating captions. There is a good balance between colour and tints, which is important in the creation of surface patterns.

2 The shape, size and proportions of a book are also critical factors in its design. This grid, which can be used as two columns, allows the design to have either wide outer margins or a large, central column space. Permanent design features such as the outer border rules can be indicated on the grid.

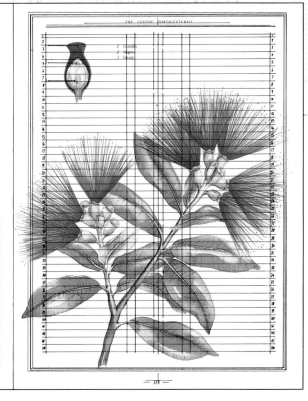

METROSIDEROS EXCELSA
Pohutukawa; New Zealand Christmas Tree

THIS large New Zealand native evergreen features prominently in Maori mythology. Early migration legends tell how the first Polynesian migrants to Aotearoa (New Zealand) saw *Metrosideros excelsa's* spectacular red blossoms while still out to sea, later christening this coast-loving and salt-resistant species pohutukawa, which means 'spray sprinkled'. The pohutukawa is also associated with death. A massive specimen that grew at Cape Reinga, New Zealand's most northerly point, was believed to be the place of departure for spirits entering Reinga, the Maori underworld. Known as Aka of Reinga, this tree sent a branch far out over the water to which exiting souls clung before taking their final plunge into the hereafter. This branch was said to have broken off during the 1820s when incessant intertribal warfare produced such bloodshed that it was unable to support the weight of departing warriors. When the great New Zealand plant hunter Thomas Cheeseman visited the site in 1895 he found only a whitened stump.

Famed for its hard, durable wood and sometimes used for boat building and furniture making, *M. excelsa* thrives in warm, frost-free coastal locations such as the northern part of New Zealand's North Island or the temperate shores of Australia. Besides being adapted to salt conditions it is also remarkably impervious to city pollution. The pohutukawa produces masses of scarlet flowers with gold-tipped stamens in dense clusters resembling bottlebrush spikes in late spring and early summer, hence its colonial name, the New Zealand Christmas Tree. It has rounded dark-green leaves with velvety silver-white undersurfaces, dark woody bark which often produces masses of brown or orange aerial roots (which, as they never anchor the tree to the ground, apparently serve no function) and a twisting root system that digs deep into the ground, sometimes enabling the tree to thrive in seemingly impossible locations such as cliff faces. *M. excelsa 'Aurea'* has pale yellow flowers.

CULTIVATION

M. excelsa can be grown in a pot from cuttings taken in late autumn or winter and transported to fertile well-drained and well-composted soil at any time of the year. It is generally resistant to pests and diseases and should be fed with a slow-release fertilizer specially formulated for native plants or a small amount of blood and bone in spring. Suitable as a free-standing tree or as a hedge, *M. excelsa* should be pruned after flowering to maintain shape and protected from frost for the first three years in colder regions.

FEATURES

Height: 3m at 10 years; 8m at maturity
Flowering period: Late spring to early summer
Colour: Scarlet

3 The layout of these pages shows how the outer margins give an excellent feeling of space, while the border around the page acts as an outer grid for both the illustrations and the text.

General design

MANY DESIGN PROJECTS require a compositional grid. Even the positioning of a logo and address within a letterhead or general stationery design can benefit from starting with a grid structure. Dividing the design space into given measurements allows the layout of the elements to be aligned to create a harmonious pattern.

The design of a company's livery when the logo and information need to be presented in a way that is consistent with the stationery, should be explored using the same grid formula as has been applied to the stationery layout.

From a basic two-dimensional design project to the development of a large, complex three-dimensional design, such as an exhibition stand, the use of grid formulae will help the designer to fulfil the potential of his brief through carefully and creatively exploiting the design devices at his disposal. The display panels or areas of an exhibition stand should be considered as design spaces in the same way as any of the other areas I have mentioned.

The creation of uniform and consistent design layouts for each of the panels will enable you to strike a balance and achieve a visual relationship between one part of the stand and another. Even the positioning of furniture and plants and the lighting arrangements can be governed by a formula.

It is important that your designs have a deliberate force that is both evidently intentional yet personal to you.

■ **1** Typing a well-laid out letter requires careful thought about spacing and margins. When you design stationery, therefore, it is essential to take account of the grid to be used for the typewritten matter, and you might even give instructions on how this should be done in relation to the design you have created. Each part of a letter should comply with certain requirements – for instance, the position of the address must line up with the window in an envelope. Other factors, too, will no doubt influence the design space and the most effective layout within this shape.

	NETT	VAT	TOTAL	

INVOICE NO.
INVOICE DATE

f

**FAITH AND
COMPANY**

**Architects
Surveyors**

3 THE SQUARE
RIVERHEAD
SEVENOAKS
KENT
TN13 2AA
TEL: 0732 460390
FAX: 0732 460302

FAITH AND COMPANY
(SEVENOAKS) LTD
REGISTERED
IN ENGLAND 2192756
VAT REG NO. 425 2992 41

2 When a stationery design has been formulated, it can be tested for its range of uses. Careful calculation or the use of a structured grid will overcome problems that can be experienced on more functional pieces of corporate documentation. You can see how the company design comfortably slots into the layout of the invoice seen here.

1 There is no area of design that cannot benefit from a compositional grid structure. This record sleeve design makes obvious use of the 45° angle grid, which leads in from the right-hand side. By deliberately flouting conventional and obvious formulae, the designer has achieved a thrusting and dynamic layout. A subtle margin around the edges of the design acts as a slightly restraining influence.

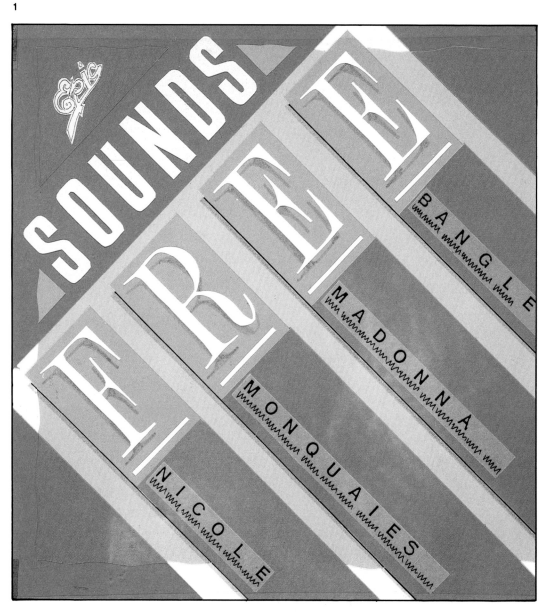

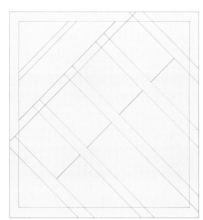

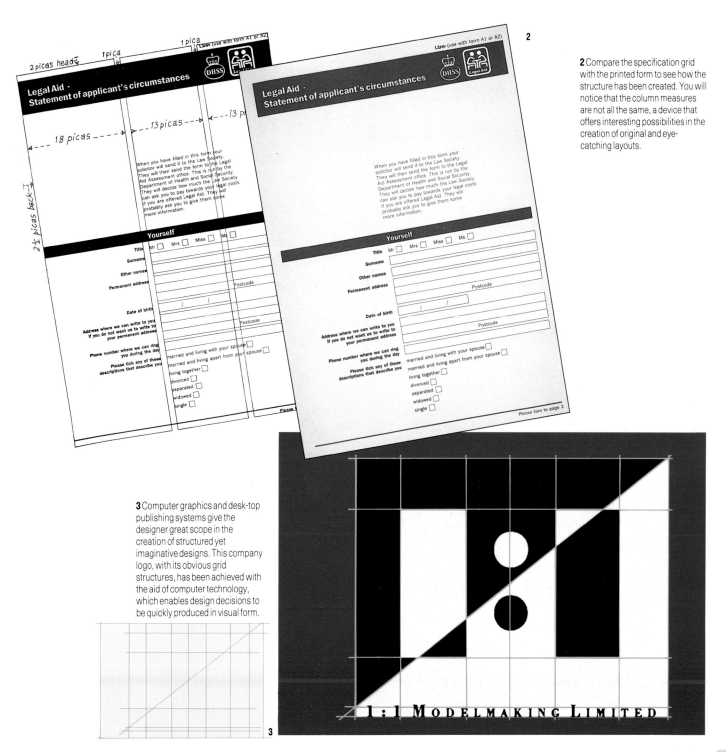

2 Compare the specification grid with the printed form to see how the structure has been created. You will notice that the column measures are not all the same, a device that offers interesting possibilities in the creation of original and eye-catching layouts.

3 Computer graphics and desk-top publishing systems give the designer great scope in the creation of structured yet imaginative designs. This company logo, with its obvious grid structures, has been achieved with the aid of computer technology, which enables design decisions to be quickly produced in visual form.

THE EFFECTIVE USE OF GRIDS

IN THIS SECTION of the book we will look at one area of the design industry and examine the make-up and construction of pages for an internationally known magazine. This rare opportunity to glimpse over the shoulder of the magazine's designer, as the thought processes develop and ideas for layout emerge, will greatly assist your understanding of the professional function of the designer's grid.

Before embarking on a visual journey, however, you must always remember that, in the case of magazine design, the styling and grid format are rigorously controlled. The magazine's proprietors will jealously guard the image they have created, both for the sake of the magazine and for the existing readership. All magazines have, intentionally or by chance, established a circulation and a share of the market. The proprietors are able to predict the class, status and educational level of this readership, and expectations of the magazine's overall appearance have been imposed by marketing considerations. It

is therefore the designer's daunting task to show flair and creativity without obviously changing or in any way damaging an already established formula.

Magazines, especially those that are firmly established, will have decided on the compositional grids they use at the time of the publication's launch. However, the magazine's directors will carefully monitor market trends to assess the effects that modern graphic design has on their product. It is, in fact, their duty to ensure that their product remains a stylish leader in its market sector. Fashions change rapidly, and typographic styles move in and out of fashion almost as regularly as clothing fashions change. Even photographic styles are carefully monitored to ensure that they are in step with the readership's expectations.

The combination of the proprietor's concern for his business and the designer's knowledge and enthusiasm to stay at the top of his profession will generate healthy and stimulating discussions about the art direction of the magazine. Steering a magazine through generations of readers and remaining the focal point of the design industry means that even the minutest design element requires intelligent visual consideration.

Nevertheless, while all these considerations are under review, it is essential that the grid remains the solid base on which the magazine is built in order to maintain stability for the production side. The compositor who generates the body text as finished setting must have reliable parameters within which to work. The feature editors need to commission articles that are written to specified lengths, and their work is made possible by the knowledge of how many words will fit in a given grid.

On the following pages you can see how the designer uses his expertise as he considers the potential of each page in terms of its position and content. You will see how the grid gives scope for the alternative and imaginative rearrangement of the elements; how photographs are proportioned and scaled to gain the maximum effect; and finally you will see the process develop through to a final printed product.

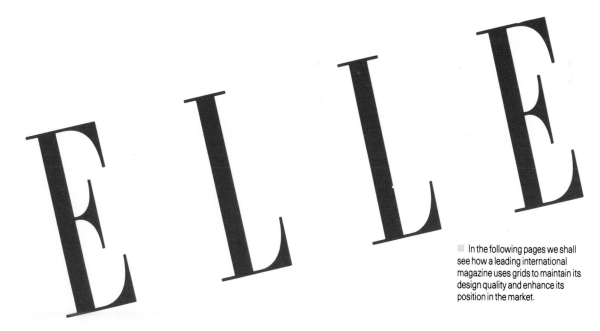

In the following pages we shall see how a leading international magazine uses grids to maintain its design quality and enhance its position in the market.

Elle magazine: case study

THIS UNIQUE MAGAZINE has evolved as a market leader. Each issue has more than 150 pages, each of which requires the individual attention of an experienced designer. Naturally, when faced with this number of pages within one journal, it is important to vary the way the layout appears. For this reason, *Elle* has devised a number of grid modules within which the designer can work.

The grids are based on the division of the magazine's contents into design-related groups. The basic options available to the designer on this magazine are three columns, four columns with a narrow margin and gutter, and four columns with a wide margin and gutter. A basic, single-column grid has been devised for the fashion section, and all of the other grids can be slotted into this overall area. Even the two kinds of four-column grid can be interlocked and used in a single design. The designer, therefore, is able to produce inventive page spread designs without having to stray from *Elle*'s own established styling.

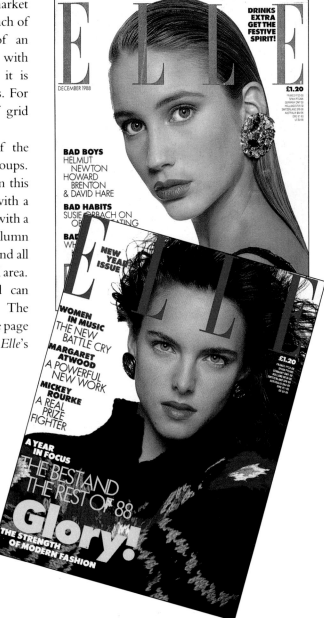

■ Although the front covers of *Elle* have no apparent grid structure, there are constraints that the designer must consider for each issue. The chief of these are the positioning and proportion of the magazine name, known as the mast-head, which always falls in exactly the same position. This, together with the typographic styling, influences the decisions made about the proportions, shape and size of the pictorial elements.

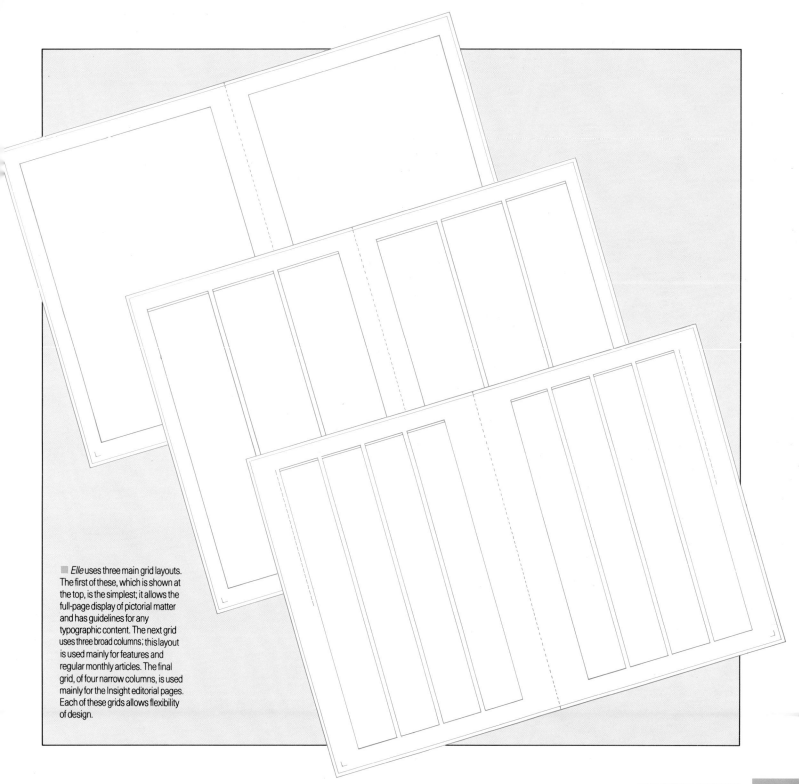

Elle uses three main grid layouts. The first of these, which is shown at the top, is the simplest; it allows the full-page display of pictorial matter and has guidelines for any typographic content. The next grid uses three broad columns; this layout is used mainly for features and regular monthly articles. The final grid, of four narrow columns, is used mainly for the Insight editorial pages. Each of these grids allows flexibility of design.

Page 1 (WRITE BACK)

WRITE BACK
LOVE IT? HATE IT? PUT IT IN THE POST!

I AM HEARTILY sick and tired of Julie Burchill's destructive attitude towards everything she touches (Patti Smith, ELLE October). Does she seriously believe that lurid political writing need always be a venomous slagging off of victims who, more often than not, never have the chance to defend themselves? Isn't she getting a wee bit old for this punkish, would-be-rebel behaviour?

Writing as an ex-admirer of her once refreshing wit, and as a critical fan of Patti Smith's, I was dismayed at Burchill's senseless attack on the latter's newfound domestic bliss. What is so terribly wrong with happiness? What is this stultifying, 19th-century attitude that says one has to suffer in order to produce good work? (I quote "...if it makes them miserable, good, they do their best work that way.") Poetic talent need not always be anchored to suffering – the refreshing element in Dream of Life is that it is not, yet still vibrant with the same rousing energy.

That Ms Burchill may loathe Patti Smith's new work is acceptable; that she feels the need to justify her opinions with pseudo-intellectual twaddle is not.
Isabel Denley
London SE18

WELL, WELL, ELLE Anglaise-style has hit the jills this time (September issue). Apart from the dreary, and very vogue-ish the interests attempt at a cosy interview with Joan Collins from Lesley White, which makes pre-teen magazines seem sophisticated, you also had ageing, ex-punkette Julie Burchill who, having quite evidently peaked an uneventful week, go-dusted an uninspired and vibric praise from the depths of her knife-drawer tot of her word of total about the moksha-day crisis.

At the end of the article the only conclusion that I managed to draw was that Ms Burchill, solely and unchallenged, would tilt the mire of truth of this discotity, especially considering that most of the so-called modern-day britches dillied by her came on in the same foregotten sea 'humble heroine' was ece bore. Whatever is the case of Jill's latest bout of ms-pd and ulmom bassically insulting journalism I doesn't speculate. But who doesn't like venus-tier bears to arms and put her good guots, energy also vastly imbroding some ms ous contains the reporting!

Maybe all ELLE tries further to represent real style ambivals out its current pseudo-trendy image, which is created off so much better by some 'youth' magazines, it will do itself and its readers a great service.
Elinor Teak
London NW4

READING AGAIN through your amusing piece 'Is She Really Going Out With Him?' brings to mind the one saying 'Love is blind'.

Perhaps I am naive and the well-known behind younger, beautiful women going out with older, ugly men is the scan of their mallets. However, perhaps it is the fact that beautiful men not only have everything handed to them on a plate from in difficult why women but don't (for the need to) to to be anything other than pretty, and actually that includes pretty selfish.

When faced with the choice between someone who may look like Tiggor from Winnie the Pooh but makes me feel centre-stand frosts and the cross between Mel Gibson and Sean Connery, who makes me feel adulated and miserable, I'll take Tiggor, thanks. At least he may not take himself so seriously as his self-indulgent counterpart.

Maybe love is not so much to do with someone's outward attractiveness as their inner beauty, in which case Pauline has probably got a pretty rare catch
Jacque Calvert
Stoke Newington

HAVING swiped my best friend's copy of ELLE from her bag one day, I was delighted to find, staring me in the face, a report about Rutger Hauer (October). I have admired his work since I first heard about him in 1981 and, despite several attempts, have never been able to find out much about him. This report in ELLE however, had information in it that I didn't know, and it was well-written and very interesting. I thank both ELLE and the reporter.

I managed to tear myself away from his picture and read the rest of ELLE which pleasantly surprised me, as I had thought up until then it was full of ads. I was wrong. I found it very interesting and I think I'll join my friend and others in clearing ELLE off the shelves every month.
C Sparkes
Southampton

IN WHAT I think was a review of Daisy Waugh's novel What is the Matter with Mary Jane? (ELLE September) Rachel Johnson made some interesting points when responding to: Her main premise throughout appears to be that overweight women should stop whining about thin models in fashion magazines and cease to regard them as culprits in the merry-go-round of anorisel eating disorders. She suggests the problem lies with 'the sufferer's fixation' with the corners own family and food. I agree that even if we were to gain upon normal bod sizes in fashion spreads, anorexia would not be in yard off the face of the earth. Eating disorders have a multitude of origins, most took with psychological and emotional problems, and clearly, the fashion world is not solely to blame. Yet to a large degree the opinion in which it belongs – the media – most certainly is, because when we consider our own appearance we are subconsciously governed by the ideal types portrayed by the media. The BBC deputy director general even on the Cambridge Diet, not doubt, for the same reason women go on it: the world more is not in keeping with the deluge of perfect images we are fed every day of our lives in the cinema, advertising and fashion spreads.

There is nothing wrong with the portrayal of thin, beautiful models selling expensive goods in fashion magazines. After all, the aim is to sell, and the product is style and image in a time when little else seems to have as much value. What is wrong is how these images make people who can never obtain them feel inadequate about their natural selves. The problem is that there seems to be a fine line between reality and fantasy in the media world and innocent people are seduced and sucked into becoming slaves one way or another, by overstaying, overeating or not eating at all.
M O'Neil
London NW2

Send your letters to:
WRITE BACK, ELLE, Rex House, 4-12 Lower Regent St, London SW1Y 4PE

---

1 This formal and precise use of the four-column grid gives you an idea of how the grid can be applied. The heading is centred on the page, with sub-headings ranged from the central column spacing. The body matter is ranged left, and the emphasis is changed visually by the weight of type. The column rules are a graphic device that give the layout a geometric symmetry.

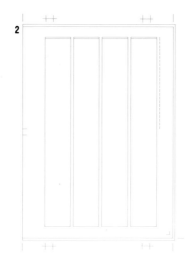

2 Here you can see the grid used for the layout of pages 1 and 3. Note how different elements of this same grid are used on these layouts.

Page 3 (insight)

insight

ELLE VINYL

● **MARY MARGARET O'HARA** *Miss America* (Virgin) Poetry 'n' emotion from Canadian new-wave folkster. Sublime.
● **ASTOR PIAZZOLLA** *Tango: Zero Hour* (Pangaea) Steamy tangos leap from the bordello to blend jazz with classical. First of a crop of fine releases from Sting's new label. Moody.
● **BOOTSY COLLINS** *What's Bootsy Doin'?* (CBS) Bass behind James Brown, ex-Funkadelic, ex-Parliament and Rubber Band shakes off the cobwebs for some weighty funk. Heavy.
● **THE HUMAN LEAGUE** *Greatest Hits* (Virgin) The sound of the early 80s. Plastic.
● **3 MUSTAPHAS 3** *Shopping* (Globestyle) Balkan beat boys burn bazooki. Fezzy.
● **JULIAN COPE** *My Nation Underground* (Island) Gleaming power pop. Shiny.
● **ANITA BAKER** *Giving You The Best That I've Got* (WEA). Smooth.
● **DWIGHT YOAKAM** *Buenos Noches From A Lonely Room* (WEA).

DESIGN
SPARTAN CRAFTS

Yet another designer-maker outlet opens this November. but Wilson and Gough 'won't be arid like an art gallery and it won't have the clutter of a crafts shop,' says proprietor

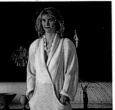

Crafty Julie (above): styling the high street

Julie Wilson Dyer Gough. Nestling amongst the sparse slate, wood and plaster of David Chipperfield Associates' architecture (as seen at Issey Miyake, Sloane St) will be 'mini individual exhibits' posed like a photographic shoot. Find Toby Russell's zig-zag platters, Anthony Bryant's wooden bowls and Sarah Simpson's real paper bowls, plus glass, metal and ceramics. EB Wilson and Gough is at 106 Draycott Avenue, SW3.

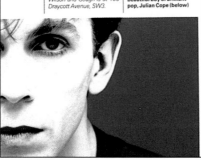

Rugged man of country. Dwight Yoakam (above): beautiful boy of brilliant pop, Julian Cope (below)

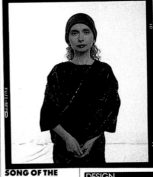

SONG OF THE STORYTELLER

'I've wanted to make this record for a very long time,' says singer **Dagmar Krause** (above). She sips coffee and talks gently in angular German tones. Having passed through pop and jazz in 70s Hamburg, various experimental music in the early 80s, and then escaped the pressures to produce pop, she has now found a vicarious home in the 30s with the mercurial German composer Hanns Eisler.

Eisler wrote over 600 songs, some in collaboration with Bertolt Brecht. It took Krause almost two years to choose and record the 22 that appear on her album, *Tank Battle* (Antilles).

A member of the German Communist Party in the 30s, Eisler fled from the fatherland's ascendant Nazism to America where he made a living scoring films in Hollywood, but was later imprisoned during the McCarthy era. Through it all, he penned some brilliant tunes.

But is it still relevant? I feel bound to ask. Krause paraphrases a line from the film *Wings of Desire*: 'When the storyteller ceases to exist, so the story will cease to exist.' She pauses. 'Eisler was writing out of the Wall Street Crash, about how if you weren't strong you were trodden on. He wrote about the racism in Germany before the war. And there are still wars. Eisler is important because playing his music is like keeping alive a story.'
ANDREW SMITH

DESIGN
COG-MAN

A passion for anything a bit mechanical encouraged **Andrew Heaps** never to put away childish things. As one of the country's few creators of automata, Heaps' enthusiasm has been rewarded by a healthy buying interest.

Heaps' work ranges from beautifully crafted animals and toys fit for the sternest Victorian nursery to the most unashamedly bawdy adult pieces such as the model of George IV being 'ridden' by one of his mistresses. 'Of course some of it is seaside humour, but if it's well executed in wood ...' says Heaps.

Andrew Heaps' automata (£15-£5,000) is available from Red Herring Studios, 24 North Place, Brighton, tel (0273) 684807.
ROBIN DUTT

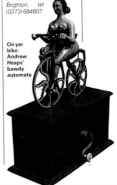

On yer bike: Andrew Heaps' bawdy automata

3 This page uses the wide outer margin guideline for the page title and for positioning a caption. This four-column grid gives the designer scope for a busy and interesting layout.

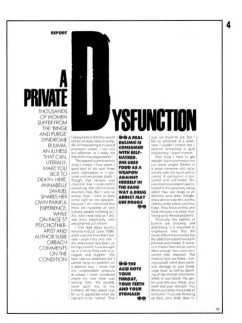

4 & 5 This page shows how flexibly the grid can be used. The design is derived from the wide four-column grid shown below (**5**), in which the second column from the right has been condensed to carry the quotations. The overall design has then been centred within the page, allowing a larger gutter and outer margin.

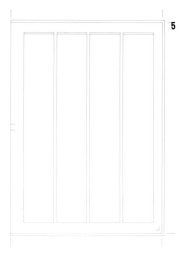

6 The formality of the three-column grid has been cunningly broken by the central overlay of a narrow four-column space for highlighting the quotation. This has been achieved by using the styling of justified copy to create the shape design. To complement this, the illustration has been used in a similar way, but its freedom has broken the formality of the page.

7 The two grids are united informally to produce the page above.

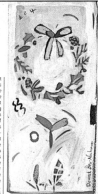

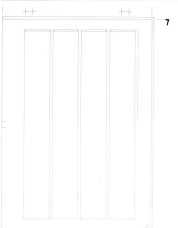

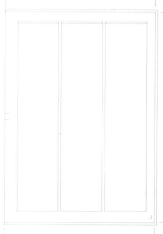

Creating the page

THE FIRST STEP is to establish the amount of copy, the heading or headings and any sub-headings, quotes or captions, and to identify any special information that needs priority. Next, the grid that is applicable to the appropriate section of the magazine needs to be chosen. The number of words in the text should be counted so that a measure of the space can be allocated to the usual type specifications. I say usual type specifications because nearly all magazines use particular typefaces set at a standard size for body matter, but giving prominence to special information.

The type specification will be marked on the manuscript, which will be handed to the compositor. Most magazines are now photo-set using computer-generated type, and it is, therefore, possible to adjust the type so that it can be accommodated in any design. Once the text is set to the specified column width, it can be used for making up the overall page design.

The space that remains when the setting is calculated is free and flexible for innovative use. The next consideration will be the photographs, heading sizes or special typographic features. These will depend on the relative volumes of the individual graphic elements, and the designer will probably work logically from the element that takes the greatest space to the one that takes the smallest. This is the easiest way to determine how best to use the available space.

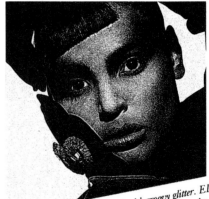

Dust up with a glittering Blush Brush, £3.90, by Loncraine Broxton. Available at Dickins & Jones, London W1; Clements Joslyn, Bishop's Stortford; The Post Box, Oxford; That's It, Sheffield; Complete Present, Cardiff; Top Of The Lane, Bolton, Greater Manchester.

Go wild with groovy glitter. ELLE predicts shimmer and shine will be the order of the night for this winter's party face, inspired by Baroque, Barbarella and the 70s. Forget Gary and the Glitter Band, and look instead to haute couture for that flash of inspiration. Lash out on false eyelashes, glittering nail varnish and star-spangled body creams.

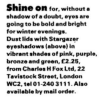

■ Each spread consists of a number of elements. These will be photographs and copy that will be set to specific design, shape and size. Typesetting can be specified so that the text creates a pleasing balance with its surrounding elements. The setting here is in a medium-weight, sans-serif face, which has been justified to create a light yet regular edge to the column. An illustration has been integrated at the base of the type to give the text a livelier, more interesting shape.

Shine on for, without a shadow of a doubt, eyes are going to be bold and bright for winter evenings. Dust lids with Stargazer eyeshadows (above) in vibrant shades of pink, purple, bronze and green, £2.25, from Charles H Fox Ltd, 22 Tavistock Street, London WC2, tel 01-240 3111. Also available by mail order.

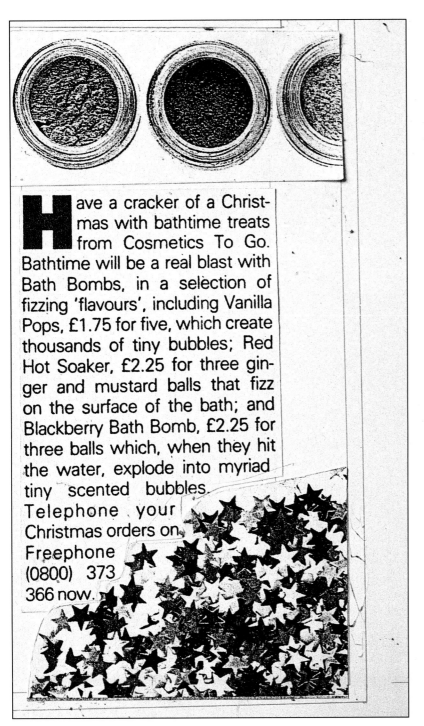

Have a cracker of a Christmas with bathtime treats from Cosmetics To Go. Bathtime will be a real blast with Bath Bombs, in a selection of fizzing 'flavours', including Vanilla Pops, £1.75 for five, which create thousands of tiny bubbles; Red Hot Soaker, £2.25 for three ginger and mustard balls that fizz on the surface of the bath; and Blackberry Bath Bomb, £2.25 for three balls which, when they hit the water, explode into myriad tiny scented bubbles. Telephone your Christmas orders on Freephone (0800) 373 366 now.

■ Modern typesetting techniques easily allow the specification of drop capitals, resembling the illuminated letters of manuscripts, which give typefaces distinction and reveal their individual design qualities.

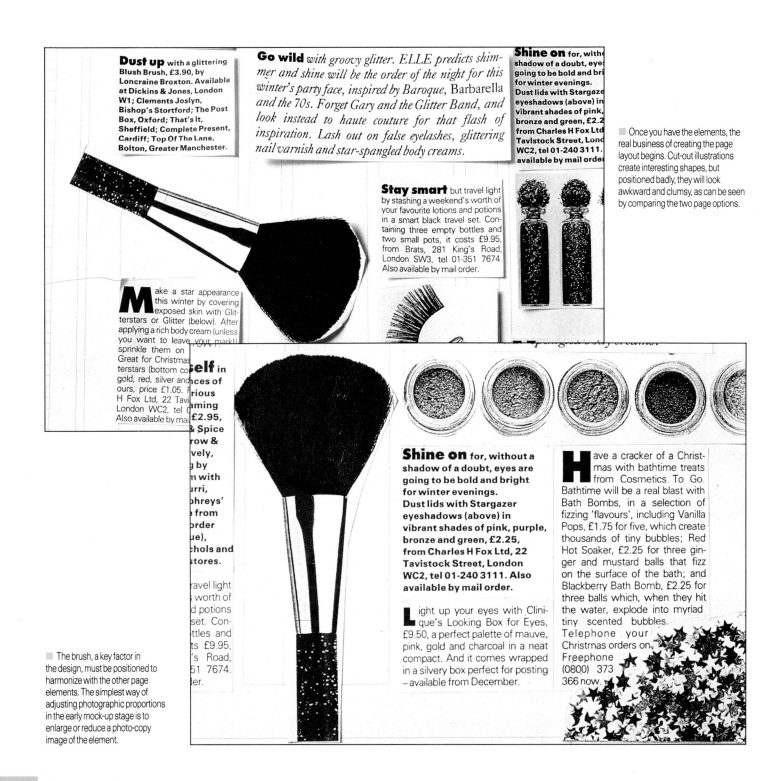

Dust up with a glittering Blush Brush, £3.90, by Loncraine Broxton. Available at Dickins & Jones, London W1; Clements Joslyn, Bishop's Stortford; The Post Box, Oxford; That's It, Sheffield; Complete Present, Cardiff; Top Of The Lane, Bolton, Greater Manchester.

Go wild *with groovy glitter. ELLE predicts shimmer and shine will be the order of the night for this winter's party face, inspired by Baroque, Barbarella and the 70s. Forget Gary and the Glitter Band, and look instead to haute couture for that flash of inspiration. Lash out on false eyelashes, glittering nail varnish and star-spangled body creams.*

Shine on for, witho[ut] shadow of a doubt, eye[s] going to be bold and bri[ght] for winter evenings. Dust lids with Stargaze[r] eyeshadows (above) in vibrant shades of pink, bronze and green, £2.2[5] from Charles H Fox Ltd Tavistock Street, Lon[don] WC2, tel 01-240 3111. available by mail orde[r]

Stay smart but travel light by stashing a weekend's worth of your favourite lotions and potions in a smart black travel set. Containing three empty bottles and two small pots, it costs £9.95, from Brats, 281 King's Road, London SW3, tel 01-351 7674. Also available by mail order.

Make a star appearance this winter by covering exposed skin with Glitterstars or Glitter (below). After applying a rich body cream (unless you want to leave your mark!) sprinkle them on [...] Great for Christmas [...] terstars (bottom co[...] gold, red, silver and [...]ces of ours, price £1.05. [...] H Fox Ltd, 22 Tavi[...] London WC2, tel [...] Also available by mai[l]

Shine on for, **without a shadow of a doubt, eyes are going to be bold and bright for winter evenings. Dust lids with Stargazer eyeshadows (above) in vibrant shades of pink, purple, bronze and green, £2.25, from Charles H Fox Ltd, 22 Tavistock Street, London WC2, tel 01-240 3111. Also available by mail order.**

Light up your eyes with Clinique's Looking Box for Eyes, £9.50, a perfect palette of mauve, pink, gold and charcoal in a neat compact. And it comes wrapped in a silvery box perfect for posting – available from December.

Have a cracker of a Christmas with bathtime treats from Cosmetics To Go. Bathtime will be a real blast with Bath Bombs, in a selection of fizzing 'flavours', including Vanilla Pops, £1.75 for five, which create thousands of tiny bubbles; Red Hot Soaker, £2.25 for three ginger and mustard balls that fizz on the surface of the bath; and Blackberry Bath Bomb, £2.25 for three balls which, when they hit the water, explode into myriad tiny scented bubbles. Telephone your Christmas orders on Freephone (0800) 373 366 now.

■ Once you have the elements, the real business of creating the page layout begins. Cut-out illustrations create interesting shapes, but positioned badly, they will look awkward and clumsy, as can be seen by comparing the two page options.

■ The brush, a key factor in the design, must be positioned to harmonize with the other page elements. The simplest way of adjusting photographic proportions in the early mock-up stage is to enlarge or reduce a photo-copy image of the element.

Photographs can be manipulated and pasted into position. Discussion on the position of type can take place and decisions be taken. Colour balances can be tested, although the photographs would be produced only in black as photocopies or PMTs at this point; they would take on the colour only at the printed stage.

Headings can be designed, typefaces can be selected, colours can be applied, information can be reversed out of solid black or even out of a vibrant colour. Rules can be run between columns to subdivide the page. Quotes can be lifted by re-setting in a larger and/or a different typeface. This is when the design really takes off.

■ **Right** The shuffling of the elements around on the grid may go through many stages before a final balance of image is achieved. Design skill is paramount in this process.

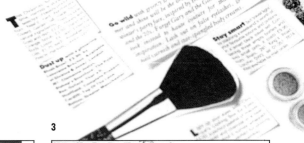

■ **1 & 3** By comparing the finished page (**1**) seen in full colour with one of the initial options (**3**) it is easy to see why the final image works.

2 Using different visual elements and the same grid, another finished page from the magazine.

1

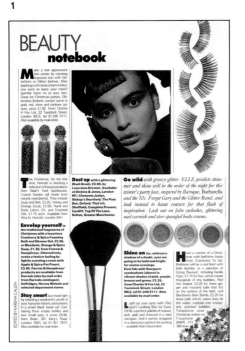

2

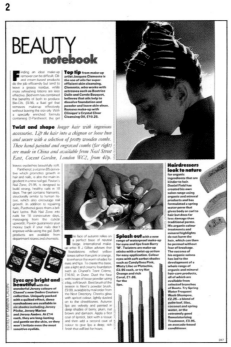

3

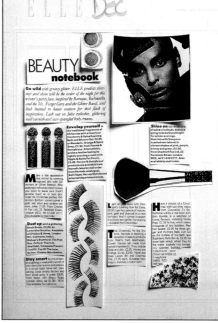

Sizing and cropping photographs

ONCE A SIZE has been established for the photographs within the grid, the pictorial aspects of the subject can be creatively manipulated to the greatest advantage.

Sometimes you will be able to work from the actual photograph. When a geometric size has been initially established, and represented by a light outline indication, normally produced in pencil or fine blue pen, it is easy to work out the actual picture image using two interlocking L-shaped pieces of card. This device enables you to adjust the size of the subject in proportion to the scale of the image. It also allows you to make compositional decisions such as zooming in and out of the image, moving from side to side or isolating a part of the photograph.

When you have established a formula, you can make photocopies or take PMT prints of the composition you have selected. These can be arranged with the text to provide a balance that gives the page character and style.

Remember that photographs should be used with

flexibility and imagination. Consider the subject matter as an outline shape and you will see the effect it has alongside the more geometric angles created by the type. You should also consider the tonal weight and colour balance and ensure that they are distributed harmoniously over the page.

Ideas, such as setting text to straddle a curved shape image, do not have to be problems. You should loosely indicate how you want them to appear and instruct the finished artworker or compositor to rearrange setting to accommodate these features.

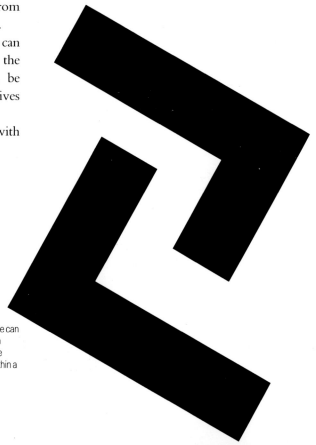

■ The two L shapes shown here can be easily cut out accurately from paper or card and used to isolate particular features or shapes within a single photograph.

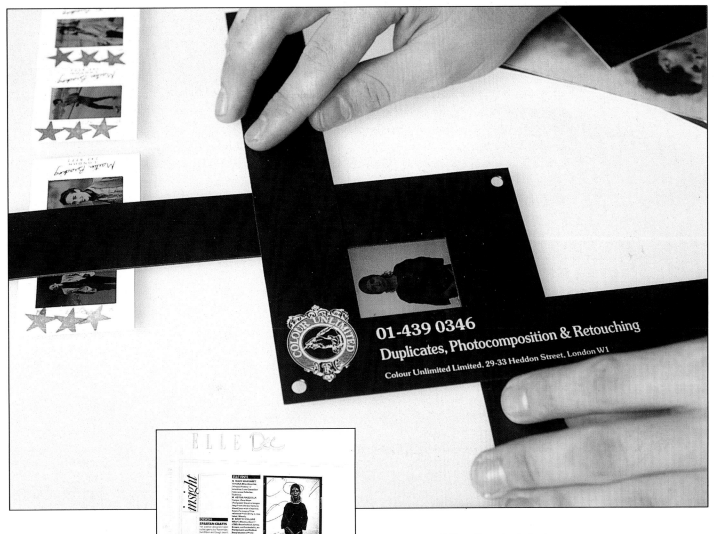

Within the image:

01-439 0346
Duplicates, Photocomposition & Retouching
Colour Unlimited Limited, 29-33 Heddon Street, London W1

Right Pictures of various shapes can be brought together within the layout and arranged to find the best balance.

Above The two interlocking Ls have been placed over a photographic transparency and moved around to make various compositional decisions. Once an appropriate cropped size has been chosen, this can be made into a rough photographic or photocopied print for the design layout.

Headings and text

HEADINGS, like photography and illustrations, can afford the designer a great deal of creative freedom, and, once again, the grid can be used as a clothes line on which letter forms can be aligned or suspended.

Elle is a good example of how type can be used in a subtle way to create a classy, illustrative style with a good deal of sophistication. A designer working on *Elle* has a wide choice of heading typestyles. Normally, condensed and linear sans serif forms are juxtaposed to give graphic balance, and colour is often liberally applied and complemented with black to create a visual reflection.

Serif faces are reserved for features such as quotes and stock page titles, so the main styling revolves around the careful use of different weights and styles of sans serif typefaces. Note how the designer often uses the column vertical as the starting point for a heading that is used among body text. Where there is the luxury of space, headings often float within this, almost giving the misleading appearance of floating without any ties to the underlying grid.

The designer has the advantage of readily available typesetting facilities, which give speedy access to different interpretations of visual typographic ideas. Colour would be tested on the design and finalized by an accurate specification to the print production department.

1

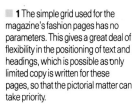 **1** The simple grid used for the magazine's fashion pages has no parameters. This gives a great deal of flexibility in the positioning of text and headings, which is possible as only limited copy is written for these pages, so that the pictorial matter can take priority.

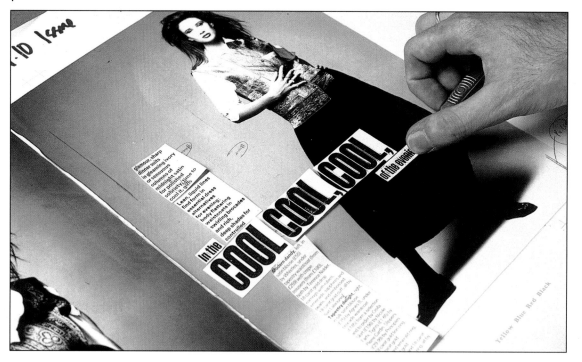

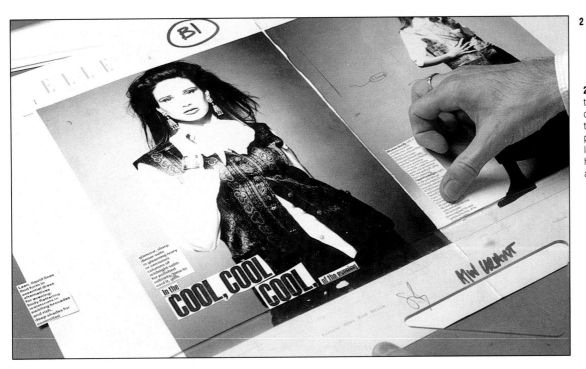

2 This heading and text will be used to describe the photographs seen over two pages. The designer therefore has the opportunity to position the written elements within a large design area. Moving the heading around enables him to make a compositional decision.

3 The elements used in this initial process have been created in black and white as rough guidelines. These will be used only to ascertain the right position. Note how the heading has been arranged to create a shape similar to that of the arm to form a visual link between the two elements.

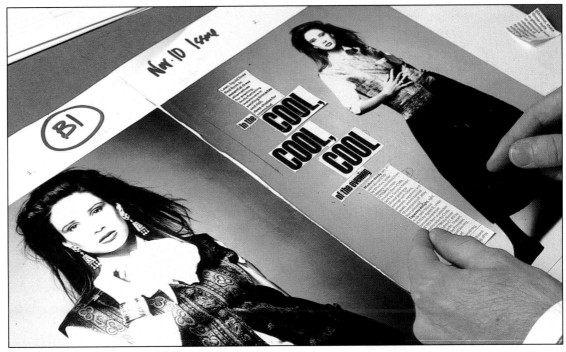

By moving these elements to exhaust all possibilities, the designer finally arrives at the right balance. This close-up shows how the heading has been used to fill the gap created by the woman's waist and arm, giving the impression of the words flowing into the picture. Below, you can see the pasted-up artwork, in which some final adjustments have been made to these positions.

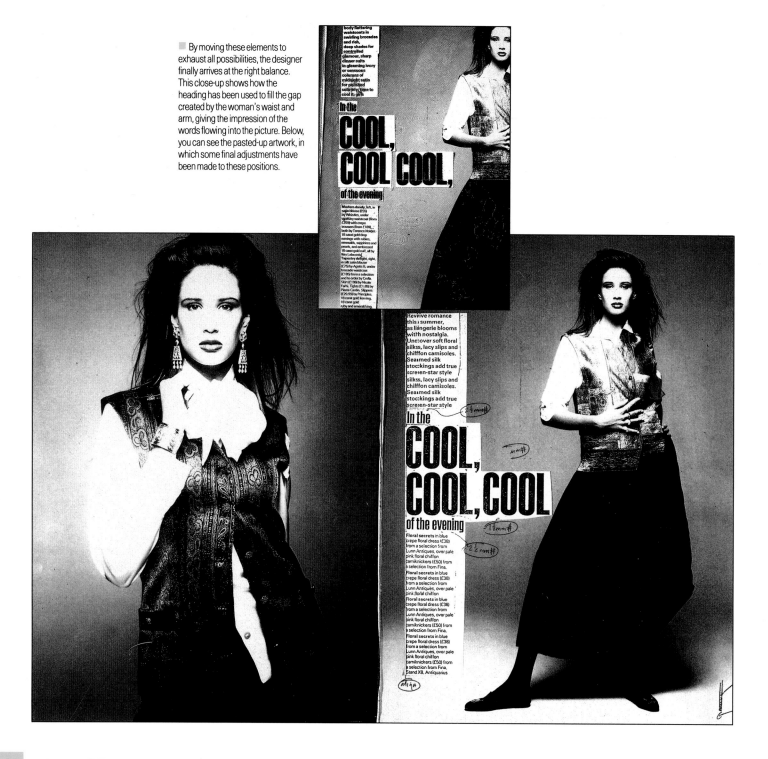

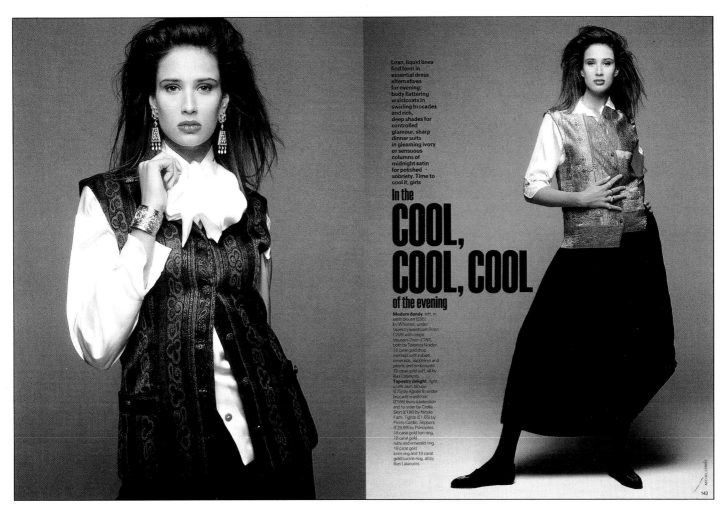

Lean, liquid lines
find form in
essential dress
alternatives
for evening;
body flattering
waistcoats in
swirling brocades
and rich,
deep shades for
controlled
glamour, sharp
dinner suits
in gleaming ivory
or sensuous
columns of
midnight satin
for polished
sobriety. Time to
cool it, girls

In the
COOL,
COOL, COOL
of the evening

Modern dandy, left, in
satin blouse (£86)
by Whistles, under
tapestry waistcoat (from
£259) with crepe
trousers (from £180),
both by Terence Nolder.
18 carat gold drop
earrings with rubies,
emeralds, sapphires and
pearls, and embossed
18 carat gold cuff, all by
Ilias Lalaounis.
Tapestry delight, right,
in silk satin blouse
(£75) by Agnès B, under
brocade waistcoat
(£185) from a selection
and to order by Crolla.
Skirt (£180) by Nicole
Farhi. Tights (£1.65) by
Pierre Cardin. Slippers
(£29.99) by Principles.
18 carat gold lion ring,
18 carat gold
ruby and emerald ring,
18 carat gold
knot ring and 18 carat
gold buckle ring, all by
Ilias Lalaounis

143

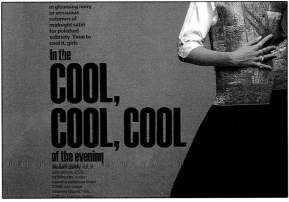

Left Studying the text and the picture more closely will allow you to see how the balance of the heading works within the shapes created by the pictorial design. The designer needs to consider, with his mind's eye, the actual printed subject to decide if the text can be produced in black, a colour, or even reversed out of a subject.

Above The printer's proof shows how the happy balance has been struck between the words and the pictorial elements. Colour in the costume predominates, while the black text and skirt merge into interesting and harmonious shapes.

Making up the page on the grid

ONCE THE ELEMENTS have been produced, photographs cropped and images established, the final page can take shape. This is when the designer decides how to use the grids that are available; whether to follow an *Elle* grid as a precise and obvious formula or whether to introduce slight shifts and mixes. For instance, you will notice examples of how the four-column grid has been shifted, with one of the columns being "squashed" to create additional space on either side of the text to give a narrow area that can be used for several purposes. This innovative design approach is used with caution and restraint, and although it adds interest to the page, it does not detract from the magazine's overall styling.

Photographs can be manipulated and pasted into position. Discussion on the position of type can take place and decisions taken. Colour balances can be tested, although the photographs would be produced only in black as photocopies or PMTs at this point; they would take on the colour only at the printed stage.

Fine detail, such as rules and graphic devices, can now be included, and the page is ready to be viewed by the Editor-in-Chief and the Art Editor.

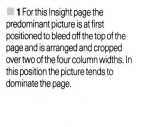

1 For this Insight page the predominant picture is at first positioned to bleed off the top of the page and is arranged and cropped over two of the four column widths. In this position the picture tends to dominate the page.

1

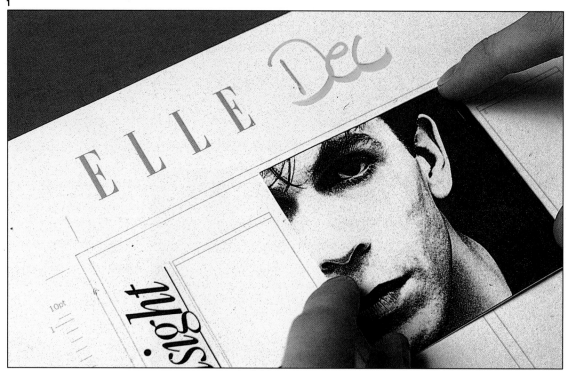

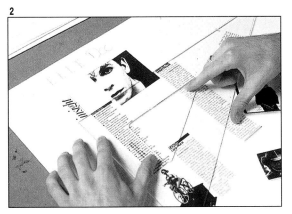

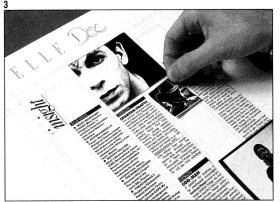

2 Text is positioned on either side of and below the picture to create a platform for the main photograph.

3 A further, smaller picture is positioned below, but it clashes dramatically and gives a top-heavy look to the layout.

4 The picture is moved to the left-hand outer column, where it is positioned to bleed off the page and act as a visual device to lead the reader into the page. Where the picture overlaps, the text can be reset to follow the line of the picture.

5 Further pictures are positioned at the bottom to balance the page. This arrangement has two functions. The first picture is an interesting shape, which breaks out of the grid, while the others are forced to occupy the space that is free from text.

6 The final spread looks rather imbalanced and clumsy, and several lines of copy have had to be cut to accommodate all the visual elements. The overall effect is busy but without harmonious balance.

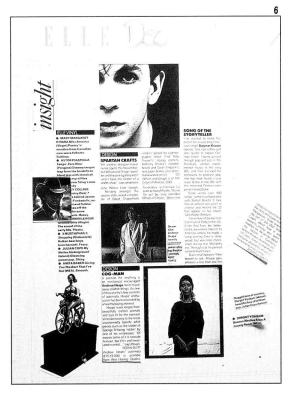

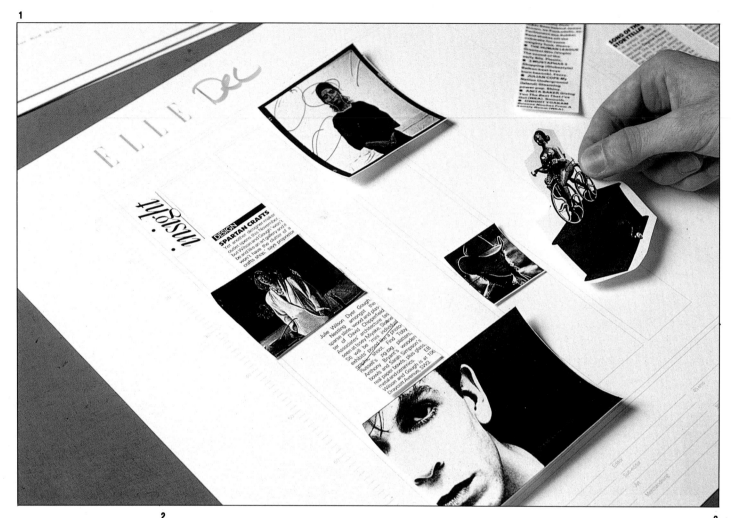

■ **1** Starting again, the pictures are rearranged into a new order. The heavy closeup portrait is brought to the bottom left of the page, providing a pedestal for further design decisions. The lighter head and shoulders picture is raised to the top right and levelled off with the top of the column of type. Further pictures are placed along a diagonal to act as breaks between the up and down effect of the columns of type.

2 Lines are drawn between the type to give the text an extra lift.

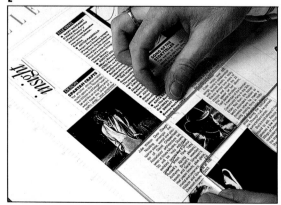

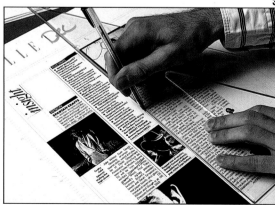

Assuming that the design requires no further work, it is ready for marking up and for technical specification. Each item of the design, from the body copy to the colour balance, requires precise specification and instruction. Weight, size and colour, along with spacing and setting instructions, would be added to the type. Notes on the colour balance and emphasis may be specified over the pictures. Rules and key lines will be described. Finally, on this particular publication, the page is signed and dated by its visual author.

Beyond the design there remain two further processes to be checked. First, the design will be made up from all the specifications into final artwork form, which requires thorough checking. This is used by the printer to produce his printing plates. Because *Elle* has such a huge print run, a colour proof would be supplied as a final means of checking for both origination errors and those created by the reprographic processes.

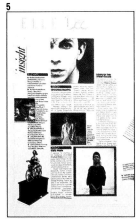

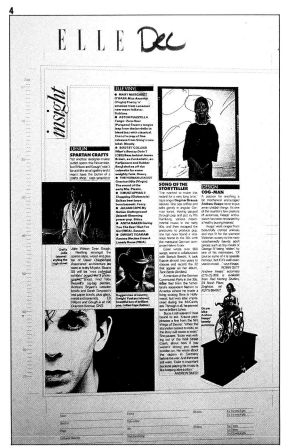

4 The final layout gives the reader the right balance of text and pictorial breaks to make a flowing rhythm of type with the occasional pause. The final paragraph ends with the ragged cut-out, which serves as a loose visual device.

5 By comparing the first attempt at the design with the one shown on this page, it is easy to grasp why the second design is more effective.

3 Copy and pictures are double-checked and aligned using a set square and fixed down into position.

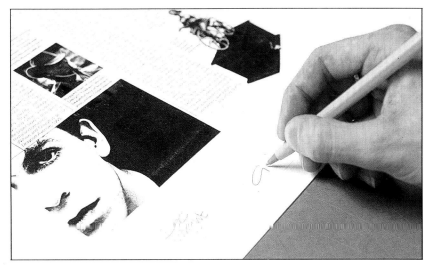

6 Once the design has been agreed, the designer commits himself to the decisions he has made by signing in the space allocated on the grid sheets.

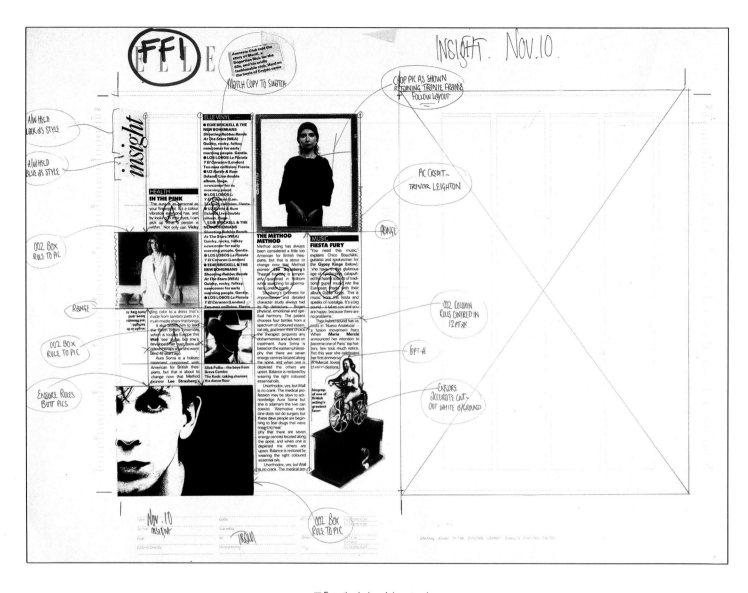

From the designer's layout and visual, artwork can now be prepared. This is pasted up for the designer to make his final print specifications. Illustrated here is the designer's marked-up layout. It gives direct and specific instructions on what has to be done to the final artwork.

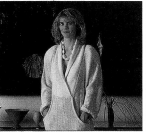

insight

DESIGN
SPARTAN CRAFTS

Yet another designer-maker outlet opens this November, but Wilson and Gough 'won't be arid like an art gallery and it won't have the clutter of a crafts shop,' says proprietor

Crafty Julie (above): styling the high street

Julie Wilson Dyer Gough. Nestling amongst the sparse slate, wood and plaster of David Chipperfield Associates' architecture (as seen at Issey Miyake, Sloane St) will be 'mini individual exhibits' posed like a photographic shoot. Find Toby Russell's zig-zag platters, Anthony Bryant's wooden bowls and Sarah Simpson's real paper bowls, plus glass, metal and ceramics.   EB Wilson and Gough is at 106 Draycott Avenue, SW3.

ELLE VINYL

● **MARY MARGARET O'HARA** *Miss America* (Virgin) Poetry 'n' emotion from Canadian new-wave folkster. Sublime.

● **ASTOR PIAZZOLLA** *Tango: Zero Hour* (Panqaea) Steamy tangos leap from the bordello to blend jazz with classical. First of a crop of fine releases from Sting's new label. Moody.

● **BOOTSY COLLINS** *What's Bootsy Doin'?* (CBS) Bass behind James Brown, ex-Funkadelic, ex-Parliament and Rubber Band shakes off the cobwebs for some weighty funk. Heavy.

● **THE HUMAN LEAGUE** *Greatest Hits* (Virgin) The sound of the early 80s. Plastic.

● **3 MUSTAPHAS 3** *Shopping* (Globestyle) Balkan beat boys burn bazooki. Fezzy.

● **JULIAN COPE** *My Nation Underground* (Island) Gleaming power pop. Shiny.

● **ANITA BAKER** *Giving You The Best That I've Got* (WEA). Smooth.

● **DWIGHT YOAKAM** *Buenos Noches From A Lonely Room* (WEA).

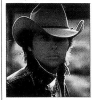

Rugged man of country, Dwight Yoakam (above); beautiful boy of brilliant pop, Julian Cope (below)

SONG OF THE STORYTELLER

'I've wanted to make this record for a very long time,' says singer **Dagmar Krause** (above). She sips coffee and talks gently in angular German tones. Having passed through pop and jazz in 70s Hamburg, various experimental music in the early 80s, and then escaped the pressures to produce pop, she has now found a vicarious home in the 30s with the mercurial German composer Hanns Eisler.

Eisler wrote over 600 songs, some in collaboration with Bertolt Brecht. It took Krause almost two years to choose and record the 22 that appear on her album, *Tank Battle* (Antilles).

A member of the German Communist Party in the 30s, Eisler fled from the fatherland's ascendant Nazism to America where he made a living scoring films in Hollywood, but was later imprisoned during the McCarthy era. Through it all, he penned some brilliant tunes.

But is it still relevant? I feel bound to ask. Krause paraphrases a line from the film *Wings of Desire:* 'When the storyteller ceases to exist, so the story will cease to exist.' She pauses. 'Eisler was writing out of the Wall Street Crash, about how if you weren't strong you were trodden on. He wrote about the racism in Germany before the war. And there are still wars. Eisler is important because playing his music is like keeping alive a story.'
ANDREW SMITH

DESIGN
COG-MAN

A passion for anything a bit mechanical encouraged **Andrew Heaps** never to put away childish things. As one of the country's few creators of automata, Heaps' enthusiasm has been rewarded by a healthy buying interest.

Heaps' work ranges from beautifully crafted animals and toys fit for the sternest Victorian nursery to the most unashamedly bawdy adult pieces such as the model of George IV being 'ridden' by one of his mistresses. 'Of course some of it is seaside humour, but if it's well executed in wood . . .'says Heaps.
ROBIN DUTT

Andrew Heaps' automata (£15-£5,000) is available from Red Herring Studios, 24 North Place, Brighton, tel (0273) 684807.

On yer bike: Andrew Heaps' bawdy automata

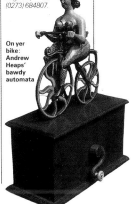

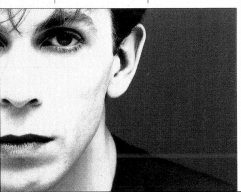

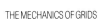

Above The finished page, shown here in its printed form, concludes this case study of grid designs in progress at *Elle*.

Left Once the artwork is complete and the designer's instructions are placed on an overlay, it is up to the printer to produce a colour proof of the final page. Minor adjustments to the colour balance can be made before the final print run.

ANALYSING GRIDS

THE DIVISION of the printed area has been influenced by many highly respected artists and intellectual designers in the 20th century. This élite group of creative pioneers developed formulae for dividing two-dimensional space and gave many designers a new vision of the balance of geometric shapes within a design area.

Le Corbusier developed a series of ideas to formulate a modular system of space design, first using the human form and its proportions for division and, later, the outward spiral of a shell and its perfect geometric relationships within a space.

These ideas form the basis of modern thinking in graphic design and have led to the exciting new developments that allow images to be displayed using numerous compositional devices.

In the design process, there is a direct relationship between the subject matter of what is to be presented and the way in which it is displayed. For instance, a simple sales leaflet, pushed through your front door, presents its information in a direct and artless way. The presentation of the complex ideas explored in,

say, an architect's journal, on the other hand, will require the intellectual and artistic manipulation of the visual matter. The extent to which your grids will contribute to your design work depends very much on the amount of research you are willing to undertake into the purposes for which the design is intended and the market at which it is directed. In most cases a simple column grid formula, as seen in the early part of this book, will form the basis for any graphic design job.

Yet whatever application your grid and design have, they will need to be interpreted as a practical vehicle for the creation of the printed subject. Once the design has been established and drawn up in rough form, a proper grid needs to be accurately drawn up. Two types of grid may be necessary. The first, produced on tracing paper, would be used by the designer to arrange the elements in the space; the second, printed on white card or paper, would be the surface on which the artwork will be positioned.

The grids for both these purposes would be printed in light-blue ink because, in the final reprographic process, light blue will not show up on the printer's photographic negative. Only the black artwork you wish to be printed will appear. Even graphic elements to be printed in colour will be drawn up in black, as the printer is able to print from your artwork to any colour you specify. The position of colour photographs and illustrations is marked on the artwork in light blue, as they are produced using a different process and the printer need only identify where they will appear.

The basic grid artwork will retain and display all the constant elements of the design. For instance, a book grid will contain a horizontal grid for type setting and a vertical grid for the columns. Special design features will be indicated, along with their alternatives. The position for folios (page numbers), information, such as running heads, which appears on several pages, and any other repeated design device will also be represented. Alternative column grids can also be featured. As much technical detail as is necessary to assist in the design and artwork process will also appear, printed around the outside.

This section of the book demonstrates the mechanics and make-up of the grid, describing each of the different parts. It shows how type is measured and applied to a grid, both manually and using computer technology, and describes in a simple and understandable way how you can use grids.

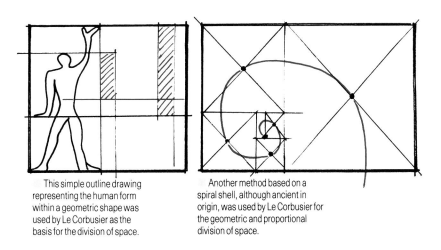

This simple outline drawing representing the human form within a geometric shape was used by Le Corbusier as the basis for the division of space.

Another method based on a spiral shell, although ancient in origin, was used by Le Corbusier for the geometric and proportional division of space.

Developing a grid

THE MECHANICS of a grid can be revealed only when it has been developed and designed, and how this is done will depend on the type of grid and on the technical practicalities attached to the job in hand. For instance, you may wish to start your grid from a purely experimental base such as those developed by Le Corbusier, Mondrian or the disciples of the great 20th-century modern art movements. Using divisions of space as linear or lateral modules, based on the mathematical and geometric division of space, you can create original and stylish pages. At some point in your design, however, you will need to look at the practical way in which the design elements can be applied within the space. If there is an abundance of text, for example, you will need to set up some logical divisions in which this matter may be displayed.

When you begin work, you will produce a number of grid designs, created in notation or thumbnail form, as the basis of your experimentation. It might be helpful to imagine that the design area is the flat plan of an empty room.

At the back of your mind you have a notional list of the items (furniture) you want to fit into this room. You intend to make this room as interesting as possible, so your choices are to place the elements (furniture) in a practical, yet harmonious, way. In your initial plans, the objects will break the space up in a clumsy, random fashion, but as your ideas of how the room can function develop, you will find ways of retaining space around the elements so that they are still practical. This will be achieved by carefully thinking about the alignment and geometric relationship of the individual elements to allow greater space for movement within the room. The grid you are about to design will structure this process as it is applied to a graphic design project.

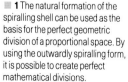 **1** The natural formation of the spiralling shell can be used as the basis for the perfect geometric division of a proportional space. By using the outwardly spiralling form, it is possible to create perfect mathematical divisions.

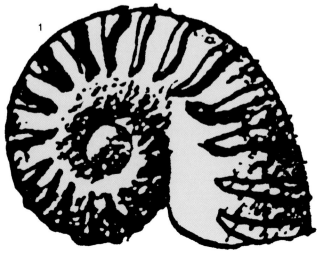

1

3

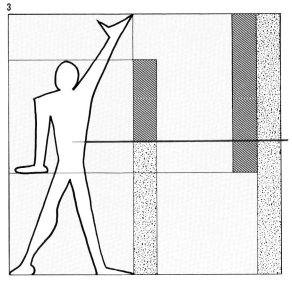

3 Le Corbusier worked on a complicated and elaborate modular system for the division of a design space, which derived from the perfect proportions of the human form. A series of complex mathematical equations developed from this form the basis of a system that reflects the Golden Section but applied with new and interesting ideas.

4

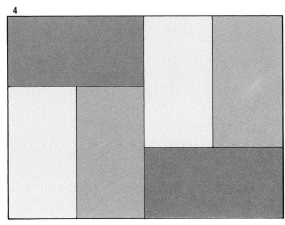

4 This simple grid, which was used in ancient Japan, derives from tatami mats and is reflected in Japanese architecture and art. It has taken several centuries for this sense of asymmetric order to filter into modern western design.

2 Determining the first point of the outward spiral will enable you to discover the first two angles of the smallest square. From this initial square the position of the larger squares can be worked out by monitoring where the spiral division runs. The centre point of each square will always fall on the spiral line, and, as they move away from the first point of the spiral, the squares will always be proportionally larger than the previous squares. The net result of this exercise is an arrangement of rectangles that is in perfect balance. This can be used as the basis for a grid, for the divisions created by the spiral can be subdivided to formulate any number of combinations.

2

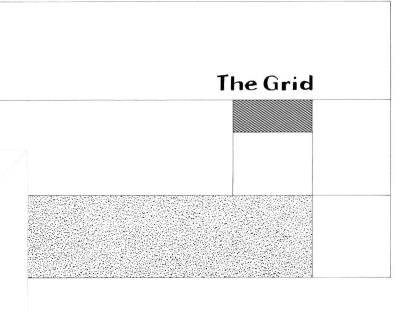

The Grid

Scaling a grid in proportion

ONCE THE GRID design has been selected from your thumbnail ideas, you will need to draw it to full size. Initially, you will need to scale up the grid as an exact interpretation of your thumbnail sketch because your thumbnail gives a glimpse of the final visual appearance of the work in hand. However, the visual qualities may become distorted as the design is produced to a larger format, and it is important to retain everything that is correct within the original idea as you draw it up into its enlarged form.

The simple formulae for scaling up and enlarging your drawings are explained in the illustration.

Having drawn up the grid to its full size, you can carefully analyse its proportions. You will need to consider the divisions between columns, margins and the head and foot of the page. You will also have to pay special attention to the gutter if the work is to be bound into pages. The visibility of the gutter will, of course, be determined by the type of binding, but in addition you should consider the effect created by the space formed by two facing gutters and balance this area with the outer margins.

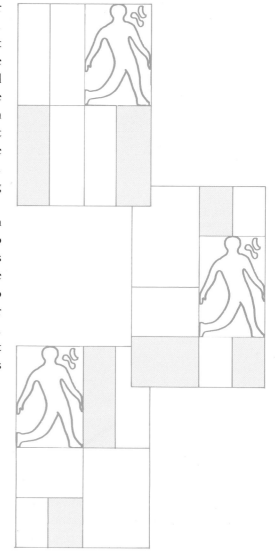

■ Some of the ideas from the modular pattern of the previous page can be explored in a number of differently proportioned designs. I have used the illustration as the key element. The tinted panels represent space, while the blank areas are used for other items.

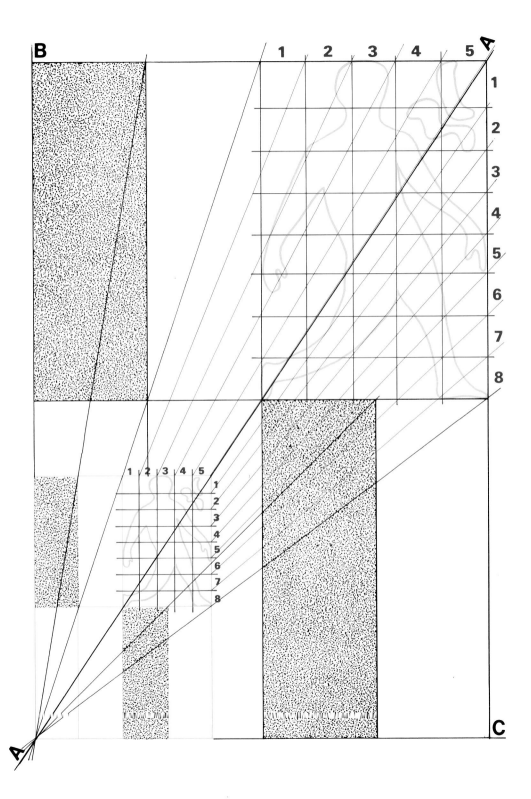

There are a number of ways you can scale your design into more finished sizes and proportions simply and quickly or create a perfect enlargement of the original form. The first is to enlarge the main overall structure. Drawing a line diagonally through your sketch, represented here by line A, will enable you to determine a new size for the enlargement. Drawing two lines, B and C, from your sketch, and then two further lines at right angles to lines B and C, meeting on line A, will create a proportional enlargement of the original shape. Further lines can be drawn from the starting point of line A through the modular divisions, and the points at which they fall on the newly drawn shape represent the new locations of those modules. To scale up more complex shapes within the design draw a grid over these shapes, scale up the grid in place and in proportion in the new design area, and transfer the features of the shape to their new positions in the larger grid.

Typography and grids

A WORKING KNOWLEDGE of typography, plus an understanding of the terminology used in type, will, at some stage in your design career, be essential. In Britain and North America, type sizes are measured using the point system, indicated as "pt". In other parts of the world, the measurement is based on the Didot point, indicated as "D". The two systems are not compatible and cannot be mixed.

A point represents a measurement of 0.351mm, and when you specify type you give the compositor a point size to work to. The type sizes most commonly used range from, say, 6pt, which you may find in the small print of contracts, to large display lettering, which may well be anything between 80pt and 150pt. The specification for magazine work may be "9pt type with a 1pt leading", which represents a vertical space of 10pts. "Leading" is the term used to refer to the measured space between lines of type. The greater the amount of leading the larger the space between lines. With a type depth scale of the kind shown on this page you can measure the horizontal rules across the columns between which the type will sit.

If you set up your divisions on the grid at 10pt intervals you can use any type of point size from 10pt downwards to fill the space. For example, you may wish to use 8pt type with a 2pt leading.

Another common system is that used to measure across the column widths – the "pica-em" measure. Six picas measure approximately one inch or 25mm. These days, however, you can easily measure your columns using millimetres only. In fact, with computer technology it is possible to use any system with which you are familiar. The computer will interpret your measurements.

2

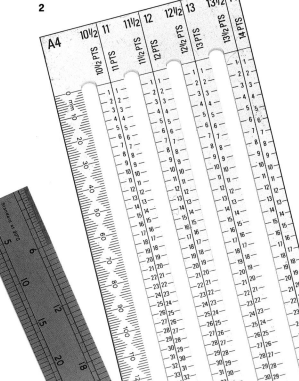

1 A type rule. This is used for measuring point sizes, especially pica-ems. One pica-em equals one 12pt measure.

2 A depth scale. This is used for measuring the space within which the type is placed. You can decide on the number of lines of type required on a page and also determine the point size of the setting to fall between these lines, although these factors will, naturally, be governed by the number of words to be included and the style of the page you are creating.

1

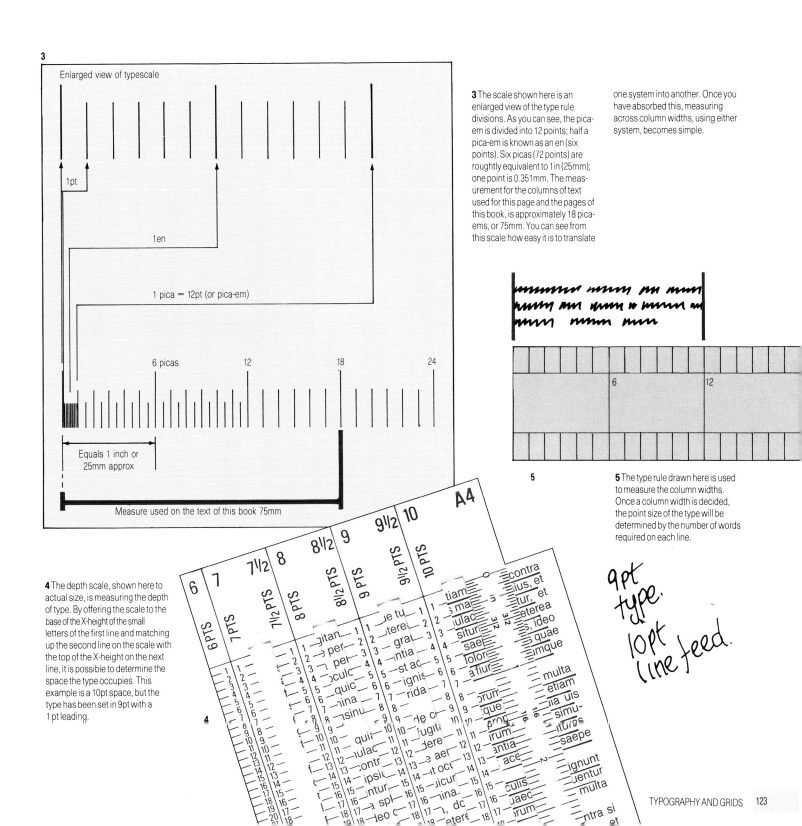

3 Enlarged view of typescale

1pt

1en

1 pica = 12pt (or pica-em)

6 picas   12   18   24

Equals 1 inch or 25mm approx

Measure used on the text of this book 75mm

3 The scale shown here is an enlarged view of the type rule divisions. As you can see, the pica-em is divided into 12 points; half a pica-em is known as an en (six points). Six picas (72 points) are roughly equivalent to 1in (25mm); one point is 0.351mm. The measurement for the columns of text used for this page and the pages of this book, is approximately 18 pica-ems, or 75mm. You can see from this scale how easy it is to translate one system into another. Once you have absorbed this, measuring across column widths, using either system, becomes simple.

5 The type rule drawn here is used to measure the column widths. Once a column width is decided, the point size of the type will be determined by the number of words required on each line.

6   12

5

9pt type. 10pt line feed.

4 The depth scale, shown here to actual size, is measuring the depth of type. By offering the scale to the base of the X-height of the small letters of the first line and matching up the second line on the scale with the top of the X-height on the next line, it is possible to determine the space the type occupies. This example is a 10pt space, but the type has been set in 9pt with a 1pt leading.

4

6   7   7½   8   8½   9   9½   10   A4

6PTS   7PTS   7½ PTS   8 PTS   8½ PTS   9 PTS   9½ PTS   10 PTS

Left typesheet (Bembo family samples):

06023 — Bembo medium/kräftig/quart-gras 8 **113** (09)

abcdefghijklmnopqrstuvwxyz
ABCDEFGHIJKLMNOPQRSTUVW
XYZ 1234567890 .,;:'" «»&!?
Håmbûrgefônstiv iam admodum mitigati raptarum animi erant sed e
arum parentes tum maxime sordida veste lacrimisque et querelis civit

33023 — Bembo medium italic/kursiv kräftig/italique quart-gras 8 **128** (09)

abcdefghijklmnopqrstuvwxyz
ABCDEFGHIJKLMNOPQRSTUVW
XYZ 1234567890 .,;:'"«»&!?
Håmbûrgefônstiv iam admodum mitigati raptarum animi erant sed earum par
entes tum maxime sordida veste lacrimisque et querelis civitates concitabant un

07023 — Bembo bold/halbfett/demi-gras 8 **145** (09)

abcdefghijklmnopqrstuvwxyz
ABCDEFGHIJKLMNOPQRSTUVW
XYZ 1234567890 1234567890 .,;:'" «»&!?
Håmbûrgefônstiv iam admodum mitigati raptarum animi erant
sed earum parentes tum maxime sordida veste lacrimisque et que

14023 — Bembo bold italic/kursiv halbfett/italique demi-gras 8 **128** (09)

abcdefghijklmnopqrstuvwxyz
ABCDEFGHIJKLMNOPQRSTUVW
XYZ 1234567890 1234567890 .,;:'"«»&!?
Håmbûrgefônstiv iam admodum mitigati raptarum animi erant sed earu
m parentes tum maxime sordida veste lacrimisque et querelis civitates co

09023 — Bembo black/fett/gras 8 **146** (09)

abcdefghijklmnopqrstuvwxyz
ABCDEFGHIJKLMNOPQRSTUVW
XYZ 1234567890 .,;:'" «»&!?
Håmbûrgefônstiv iam admodum mitigati raptarum animi erant
sed earum parentes tum maxime sordida veste lacrimisque et qu

16023 — Bembo black italic/kursiv fett/italique gras 8 **131** (09)

abcdefghijklmnopqrstuvwxyz
ABCDEFGHIJKLMNOPQRSTUVW
XYZ 1234567890 .,;:'"«»&!?
Håmbûrgefônstiv iam admodum mitigati raptarum animi erant sed ea
entes tum maxime sordida veste lacrimisque et querelis civitat

Right typesheet (point sizes):

10 on 10
abcdefghijklmnopqrstuvwxyz
ABCDEFGHIJKLMNOPQRSTUVWXYZ
1234567890&%★£$?!(),.;:'"

11 on 11
abcdefghijklmnopqrstuvwxyz
ABCDEFGHIJKLMNOPQRSTUVWXYZ
1234567890&%★£$?!(),.;:'"

12 on 12
abcdefghijklmnopqrstuvwxyz
ABCDEFGHIJKLMNOPQRSTUVWXYZ
1234567890&%★£$?!(),.;:'"

13 on 13
abcdefghijklmnopqrstuvwxyz
ABCDEFGHIJKLMNOPQRSTUVWXYZ
1234567890&%★£$?!(),.;:'"

14 on 14
abcdefghijklmnopqrstuvwxyz
ABCDEFGHIJKLMNOPQRSTUVWXYZ
1234567890&%★£$?!(),.;:'"

15 on 15
abcdefghijklmnopqrstuvwxyz
ABCDEFGHIJKLMNOPQRSTUVWXYZ
1234567890&%★£$?!(),.;:'"

16 on 16
abcdefghijklmnopqrstuvwxyz
ABCDEFGHIJKLMNOPQRSTUVWXYZ
1234567890&%★£$?!(),.;:'"

17 on 17
abcdefghijklmnopqrstuvwxyz
ABCDEFGHIJKLMNOPQRSTUVWXYZ
1234567890&%★£$?!(),.;:'"

18 on 18
abcdefghijklmnopqrstuvwxyz
ABCDEFGHIJKLMNOPQRSTUVWXYZ
1234567890&%★£$?!(),.;:'"

Above This sheet distinguishes the various point sizes in which a given typeface or style is available. Next to the type are numbers indicating the point size.

Left The typesheet shows some of the different styles of type available in a single typeface. Every typeface is part of a family that has distinctive design emphasis of weight and styling.

1

Lrem ipsum dolor sit amet, consectetur adipiscing elit, sed diam zum nonnumy eiusmod tempor incidunt ut labore et dolore magna aliqua erat volupat. Ut enim ad minim veniam, quis nostrud exercitation nisi ut aliquip ex era commodo consequat. Duis autem vel eum irure dolor in reprehenderit in volupante velit esse molestaie consequat, vel illum dolore eu fugiat nulla pariatur. At vero eos et accusam et iusto odiom dignissim qui blandit praesent luptatum delenit aigue duos dolor et se molestia

2

excepteur sint occaecat cupidtat non provident, simil sunt it culpa qui officia deserunt mollit anim id est laborum et dolor fuga. Et harumd dereud facilis est er expedit distinct. Nam liber tempor cumet soluta nobis eligend optio. Omnis dolor debi aut tum rerum necessit atib saepe evenitet ut er repudiand sint et recus Itaque earud rerum hic tenetury sapiente delectus au aut prefer endis dolorib asperiore repellat. Hanc ego cum tene senteniam, quid est cu verear ne ad eam non possing

3

accommodare nost ros quos tu paulom ante cum memorite tum etia ergat. Nos amice et nobevol, olestias non potest fier ad augendas cum conscient to factor tum poen legum odiot. Et tamewn in buisdam neque pecun modut est neque nonor imper nedet libiding gen epular religuard cupidtat, quas nulla praid onr undamte. Impro pary minuit, potius inflammad et coercend magist and et dom videantur. Invitat igitur vera ratio bene sanos ad iustitiam, aequitated fidem. Neque hominy infant aut

4

iniuste fact est cond qui neg faciletes efficerd possit duo contenud notiner si effecerit, et opes vel fortunag et ingen liberalitat magis conveniunt, da but tuntung benevolent sib con et, aptissim est ad quiet. Endium caritat praesert cum omning null sit caus peccand quaert en imigent cupidat a natura proficis facile explent sine ulla inura autend nihil enim desiders. Concupis plusque in inspinuria detriment est quam in his rebus quode emolument oariunt iniur. Itaque ne iustitial dem rect

5

quid dixer per se iucund est proptewr and tutior vitam et luptat pleniore eficit. Tia nonte ea colu in incommenod quae egnium improb fugiendad improbitates putamuy sed mult etiam mag quod cius. Lrem ipsum dolor sit amet, consectetur adipiscing elit, sed diam zum nonmumy eiusmod tempor incidunt ut labore et dolore magna aliqua erat volupat. Ut enim ad minim veniam, quis nostrud exercitation nisi ut aliquip ex era commodo consequat. Duis autem vel eum irure dolor in

6

reprehenderit in volupante velit esse molestaie consequat, vel illum dolore eu fugiat nulla pariatur.

Invitat igitur vera ratio bene sanos ad rustitiam, aequitated fidem. Neque hominy infant aut iniuste fact est cond qui neg faciletes efficerd possit duo contenud notiner si effecerit, et opes vel fortunag et ingen. Lrem ipsum dolor sit amet, consectetur adipiscing elit, sed diam zum nonnumy eiusmod tempor incidunt ut labore et dolore magna aliqua erat volupat. Ut enim ad minim

1 This typesetting depicts 9pt Bembo set within a 9pt space. When there is no extra space between the lines of type as here, it is known as setting type solid. The text has been justified, which means that it runs across the whole width of the column to create a solid slab of text, with the type running up to both left- and right-hand margins. The column width has been measured to 18 pica-ems.

2 The text has been set and justified in 9pt type in an 11pt space to allow more space between the lines.

3 This is an example of 9pt Bembo set in a 14pt space, which gives a lighter, more spacious feel to the typographic imagery.

4 Here is an example of 9pt setting, set solid but ranged left (or ragged right as it is sometimes known). To counterbalance the raggedness, paragraphs can be indented by specifying the measurement of indentation required.

5 This 9pt type in an 11pt space is ranged right (or ragged left). This arrangement creates an alternative design, and when it is used alongside ranged left setting, with the ragged edges at the outer extremes, creates a balanced and attractive visual effect.

6 Centred setting in 9pt type in a 14pt space is useful for featuring text or if there is only a single column of text to be set.

Once you have established the point size that gives your page the best visual quality, you will need to see how many characters (small letters) fit into your line measurement. You can do this by studying the typesheets supplied by your typesetter. Remember, words have spaces between them, and this is calculated by allowing one letter (or character) space between each word.

The four most common forms of setting text are ranged right, ranged left, justified and centred.

Paragraphs can be indented at the start, and large capitals can be used to make a feature of the body matter.

You will see from all this that the parallel horizontal lines on your grid will establish a quick formula for calculating the number of lines that can fit on a page within the confines of the designed structure. Where the creative skill becomes important is in the subtle shapes and tones created by the finished typesetting.

The anatomy of the grid

THE BASIC STRUCTURE of the grid design contains reference points that enable you to discuss certain design features with colleagues or clients. For example, when the word folio is mentioned in reference to a page in a sequence of pages, it is the description of the position of the page numbers, which would be already indicated on the grid. Column widths will be drawn up on this grid, with the possible addition of optional column widths around the edges, and other design features, such as margins, gutters, column divisions, indicators for headings or graphic devices, will also be included.

Another feature of your grid is the outer size of the design area and the crop size of the finished page or design. The outer size is an extra margin, normally about 3mm wide, which is known as the bleed. This is present for overlapping areas of colour or illustrative matter that run off the page, and it is used as a safety margin when the page is trimmed after printing. The illustration or colour is printed over the area that will be cut so that when it is trimmed to size there will be no danger of the unprinted paper showing as a white edge. The marks that are used to guide the cutting are known as the cropping marks, and are found inside the bleed.

Always remember that the main characteristic of any grid should be the ease with which it can be used. For this purpose, the ruled lines for body copy can be shown, together with the exact number of type lines to appear on a page. If the grid is to carry more than one range of point sizes, the alternative size can be placed in the outer artwork margin to make it easy to locate the printed typesetting for pasting in position. You will be able quickly to establish the exact space the type is likely to occupy, and it will also give you the flexibility to move it around.

Overleaf you can see the grid used for this book. The marginal notes explain the grid's function and the many options it offers the designer.

1

Running head

Head margin

Back margin

Fore-edge margin

Crosshead

Foot note

Folio

Measure

1 Just as the human body has its own anatomy, so the page layout or design can be described with its own physical features. This example shows the typical terms used to identify the various parts of the page.

2

Caption

Heading

Introduction

Bold run in

Indent

Column rule

Foot margin

2 The grid should serve as a flexible tool to aid in the design process. It is up to the designer to incorporate all possible contingencies, whether or not they are apparent in the early design stages. In this way, the artworker can easily and quickly follow all of the design instructions. This diagram shows some of the recurring features present in the design of a magazine spread.

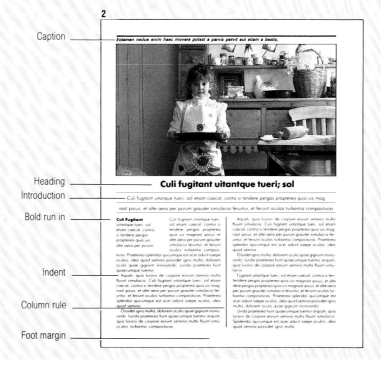

Culi fugitant uitantque tueri; sol

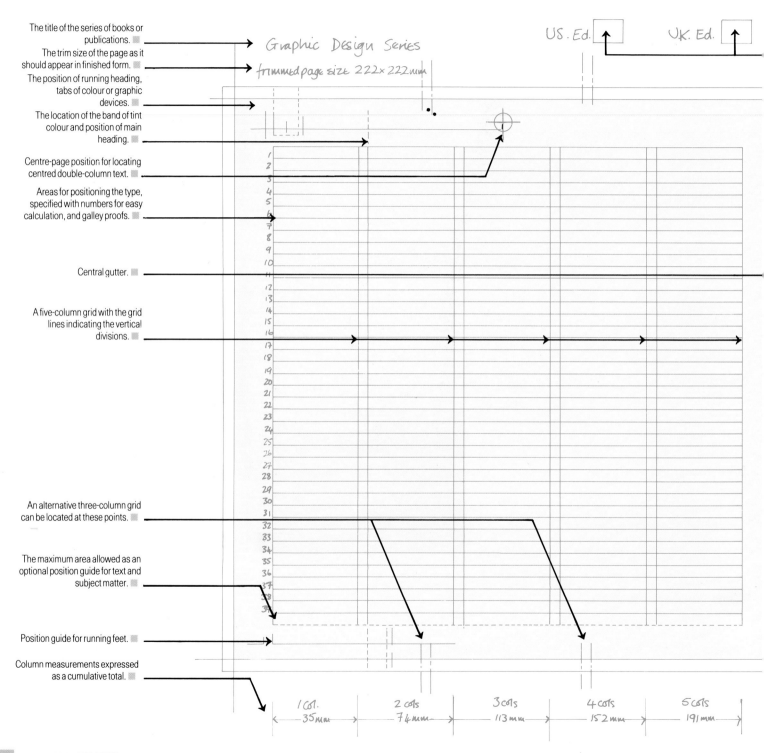

The title of the series of books or publications. ▨

The trim size of the page as it should appear in finished form. ▨

The position of running heading, tabs of colour or graphic devices. ▨

The location of the band of tint colour and position of main heading. ▨

Centre-page position for locating centred double-column text. ▨

Areas for positioning the type, specified with numbers for easy calculation, and galley proofs. ▨

Central gutter. ▨

A five-column grid with the grid lines indicating the vertical divisions. ▨

An alternative three-column grid can be located at these points. ▨

The maximum area allowed as an optional position guide for text and subject matter. ▨

Position guide for running feet. ▨

Column measurements expressed as a cumulative total. ▨

Graphic Design Series

trimmed page size 222 × 222 mm

US. Ed.   U.K. Ed.

1 col.   2 cols   3 cols   4 cols   5 cols
35mm   74mm   113mm   152mm   191mm

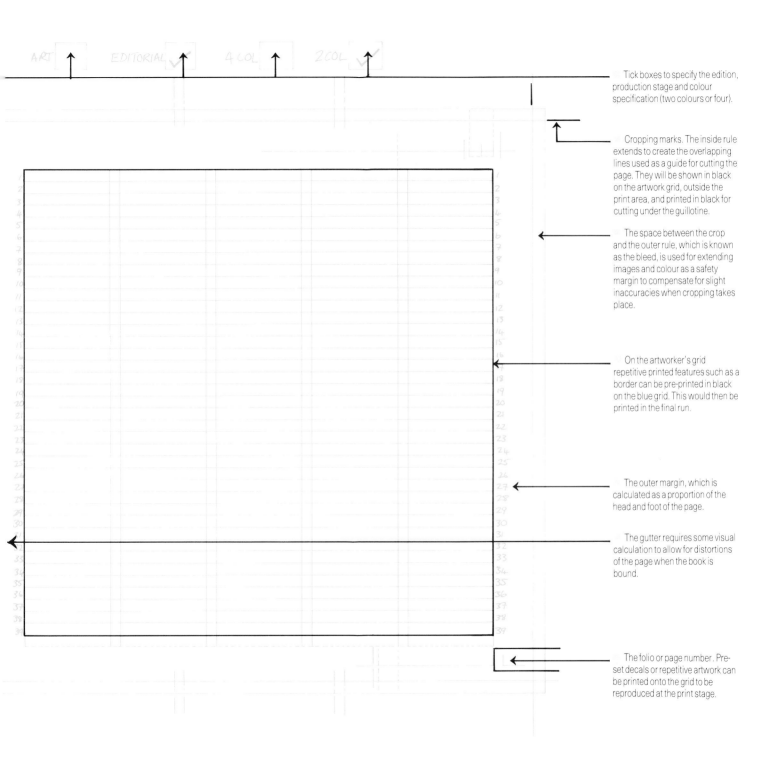

ART EDITORIAL ✓ 4 COL 2 COL ✓

Tick boxes to specify the edition, production stage and colour specification (two colours or four).

Cropping marks. The inside rule extends to create the overlapping lines used as a guide for cutting the page. They will be shown in black on the artwork grid, outside the print area, and printed in black for cutting under the guillotine.

The space between the crop and the outer rule, which is known as the bleed, is used for extending images and colour as a safety margin to compensate for slight inaccuracies when cropping takes place.

On the artworker's grid repetitive printed features such as a border can be pre-printed in black on the blue grid. This would then be printed in the final run.

The outer margin, which is calculated as a proportion of the head and foot of the page.

The gutter requires some visual calculation to allow for distortions of the page when the book is bound.

The folio or page number. Pre-set decals or repetitive artwork can be printed onto the grid to be reproduced at the print stage.

Artworking a grid

FORMALIZED PRINTED GRIDS simplify the design process, speeding and easing both the production of a piece of design work and the completion of the artwork. The designer uses printed grids for two basic reasons. First, because the technical structure and format are already in place in the form of position guides, margin sizes and so on, he or she can quickly and accurately work around the established detail. Second, because the designer need not worry about these details, he or she is free to devote creative resources and energy to arranging the graphic elements.

The grids will probably be printed in light blue ink on a translucent surface so that they can be used to trace over letter forms or illustrations, to paste up the graphic elements and as a drawing surface.

The person who completes the artwork requires the same grid, drawn up with the same amount of detail and to the same degree of accuracy, and it will probably be the artworker's task initially to create the artwork for the grid itself. This will be done in the same way as any design job – the designer will supply the artworker with the exact specifications for the grid. The artworker will also receive any instructions for special requirements such as logos, box rules or graphic devices that can be pre-printed as artwork in black and used in the final print. The rest of the grid will be printed in blue, as this will not be reproduced but used only as a guide. Remember that, for technical reasons, light blue does not appear on the printer's negatives when the printing plates are made.

■ The artwork for the grid will be drawn up in black using different sized technical pens. The artwork will be drawn accurately to the exact size it is to be printed and will be marked up for printing in blue, with any special black features picked out.

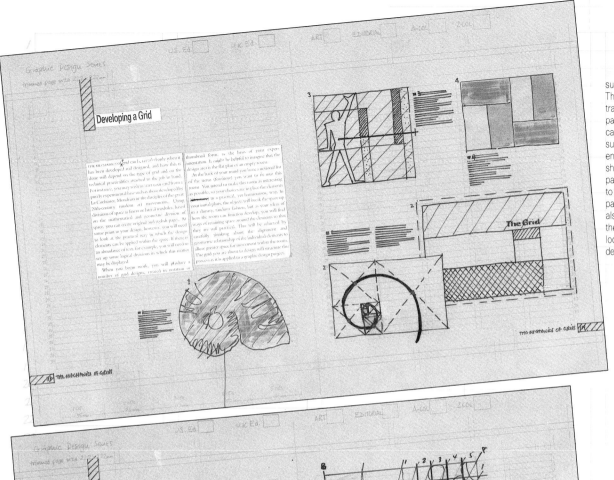

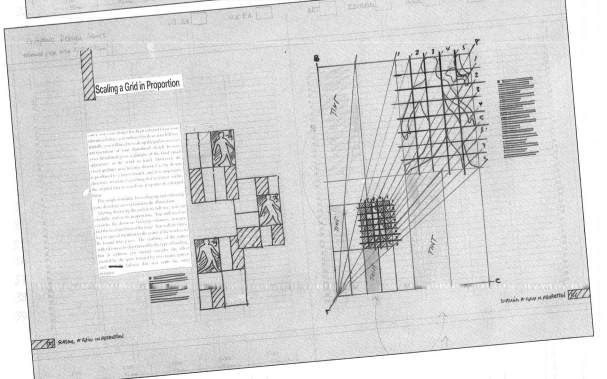

The designer will specify the surface he requires for his grids. These are often printed on a translucent detail paper or tracing paper so that the design elements can be projected through the surface with the aid of a light box or enlarger. The two design layouts shown here were produced for pages in this book, and passed on to the artworker who made up the pages on thin white board, which also has the printed grid. These are then despatched to the printer, who locates all the elements from the design layout and the artwork.

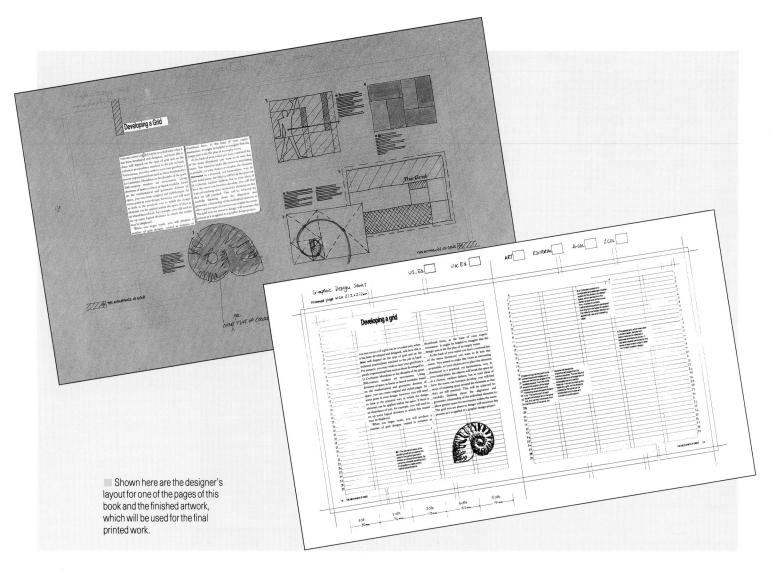

Shown here are the designer's layout for one of the pages of this book and the finished artwork, which will be used for the final printed work.

When the artworker draws up the initial master grid, he will use black ink, which will be marked up for the printer to reproduce in blue, although some features may be marked to be printed in black. The artworker's grids will normally be on a thin, high-quality card with a treated surface, so that any errors can be scratched off with a sharp blade.

The artworker will then take the designer's layouts, which have been completed on translucent grids, to make up the finished artwork on his printed grids, following the design and instructions on the designer's layouts. The finished artwork is given to the printer as camera-ready copy for the reproduction process.

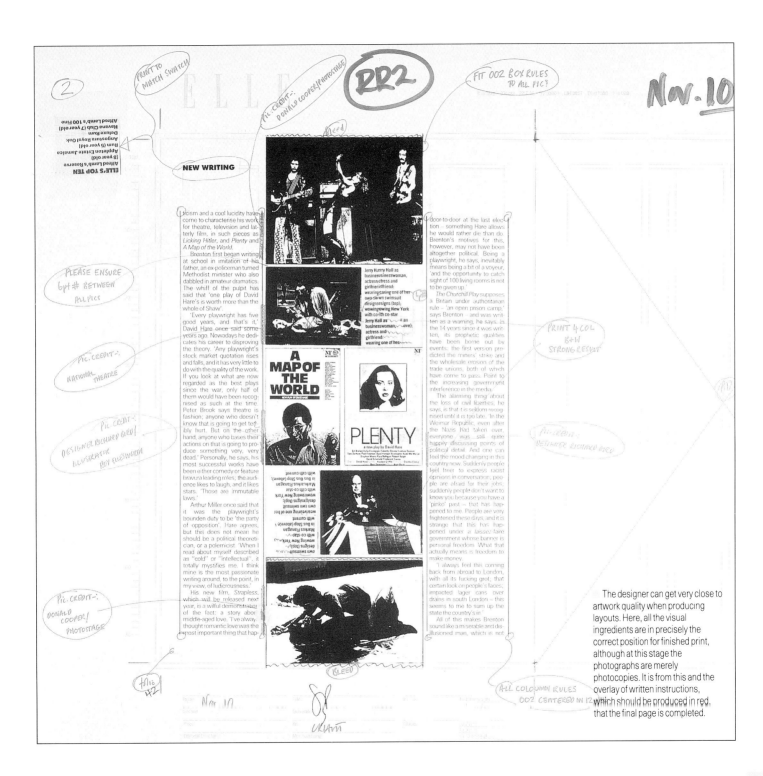

RR2

PRINT TO MATCH SWATCH

PIC. CREDIT:- DONALD COOPER/PHOTOSTAGE

FIT 002 BOX RULES TO ALL PICS

ELLE

NEW WRITING

PLEASE ENSURE 6pt # BETWEEN ALL PICS

PIC. CREDIT:- NATIONAL THEATRE

PIC. CREDIT:- DESIGNER RICHARD BIRD/ ILLUSTRATOR ROY ELLSWORTH

PIC. CREDIT:- DONALD COOPER/ PHOTOSTAGE

PRINT 4 COL B+W STRONG RESULT

PIC. CREDIT:- DESIGNER RICHARD BIRD

ticism and a cool lucidity have come to characterise his work for theatre, television and latterly film, in such pieces as *Licking Hitler*, and *Plenty* and *A Map of the World*.

Brenton first began writing at school in imitation of his father, an ex-policeman turned Methodist minister who also dabbled in amateur dramatics. The whiff of the pulpit has said that 'one play of David Hare's is worth more than the whole of Shaw'.

'Every playwright has five good years, and that's it,' David Hare once said some years ago. Nowadays he dedicates his career to disproving the theory. 'Any playwright's stock market quotation rises and falls, and it has very little to do with the quality of the work. If you look at what are now regarded as the best plays since the war, only half of them would have been recognised as such at the time. Peter Brook says theatre is fashion; anyone who doesn't know that is going to get terribly hurt. But on the other hand, anyone who bases their actions on that is going to produce something very, very dead.' Personally, he says, his most successful works have been either comedy or feature bravura leading roles; the audience likes to laugh, and it likes stars. 'Those are immutable laws.'

Arthur Miller once said that it was the playwright's bounden duty to be 'the party of opposition'. Hare agrees, but this does not mean he should be a political theoretician, or a polemicist. 'When I read about myself described as "cold" or "intellectual", it totally mystifies me. I think mine is the most passionate writing around, to the point, in my view, of ludicrousness.'

His new film, *Strapless*, which will be released next year, is a wilful demonstration of the fact: a story about middle-aged love. 'I've always thought romantic love was the most important thing that hap-

Jerry Herry Hall as businesbusinesswoman, actressactress and girlfriergirlfriend: wearingwearing one of her own-swn swimsuit designsesigns (top); wowingrowing New York with co-th co-star Jerry Hall as ... an businesswoman, ... ve); actress and girlfriend: wearing one of hes-

A MAP OF THE WORLD
NEW PLAY BY DAVID HARE
NT

PLENTY
a new play by David Hare

Markaltus Flanagan in Bus Stop (above), with co-star wowingwring New York designesigns (top); own swn swimsuit with current Markus Flanagan in Bus Stop (above), with co-star

door-to-door at the last election – something Hare allows he would rather die than do. Brenton's motives for this, however, may not have been altogether political. Being a playwright, he says, inevitably means being a bit of a voyeur, 'and the opportunity to catch sight of 100 living rooms is not to be given up.'

The Churchill Play supposes a Britain under authoritarian rule – 'an open prison camp,' says Brenton – and was written as a warning, he says. In the 14 years since it was written, its prophetic qualities have been borne out by events: the first version predicted the miners' strike and the wholesale erosion of the trade unions, both of which have come to pass. Point to the increasing government interference in the media.

The alarming thing about the loss of civil liberties, he says, is that it is seldom recognised until it is too late. 'In the Weimar Republic, even after the Nazis had taken over, everyone was still quite happily discussing points of political detail. And one can feel the mood changing in this country now. Suddenly people feel freer to express racist opinions in conversation; people are afraid for their jobs; suddenly people don't want to know you because you have a 'pinko' past – that has happened to me. People are very frightened these days, and it is strange that this has happened under a *lassez-faire* government whose banner is personal freedom. What that actually means is freedom to make money.

'I always feel this coming back from abroad to London, with all its fucking grot; that certain look on people's faces; impacted lager cans over drains in south London – this seems to me to sum up the state the country's in.'

All of this makes Brenton sound like a miserable and disillusioned man, which is not

folio #2

Nov. 10

ALL COLUMN RULES 002 CENTERED IN 12

The designer can get very close to artwork quality when producing layouts. Here, all the visual ingredients are in precisely the correct position for finished print, although at this stage the photographs are merely photocopies. It is from this and the overlay of written instructions, which should be produced in red, that the final page is completed.

Desk-top publishing

EACH YEAR brings advances in technology, and computers are now playing a major role in the communication of words and images with speed and precision. Certain areas of design, especially those in the publishing industry, are rapidly introducing new systems. Designs for pages need no longer be produced as rough layouts and translated by artworkers, since both these operations can now be combined as a single activity. These new systems are, however, reliant on good design structure, and as desk-top publishing is available to anyone, most systems have in-built grid designs for the inexperienced operator.

For the more advanced visual creators, computers are flexible tools, allowing information to be displayed on a monitor and manipulated into various alternative design formulae. The great advantage of this technology is the reduction of hand skills required in the design process. Type images can be selected and displayed on the screen; photographs and illustrations can be captured by a video camera; reductions and enlargements of all the graphic elements can be manipulated by a single action; and any specified colour can be included.

Print-outs can be produced as the basis for discussion at design meetings, and discs that are compatible with the technology of the printer can be used in the final print process.

In short, some areas of design will be made easier and less labour-intensive in future years. However, the factors that can never be replaced by technology are the skill and creative imagination of the designer's mind and eye.

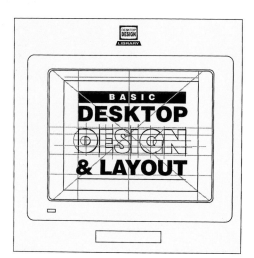

1 Linear shapes and forms can be quickly established on the monitor screen by operators who have no formal art training. Images can be projected into the design, and grids can be formulated for locating the elements. Pre-set grids are often available if special graphic programs are bought.

2 Advances in computer technology make it possible to mix colours from the palettes included in the graphic programs, and selected colours can be quickly stripped into the experimental designs. Artwork can be produced from the information that has been created by the operator, thereby obviating the need to involve skilled artworkers in the make-up process. In order to do this well, however, you need an extensive and full knowledge of all aspects of graphic design.

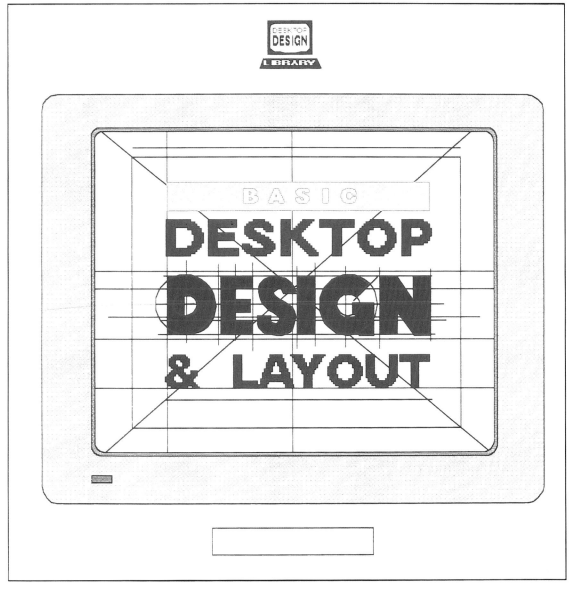

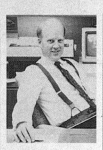

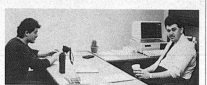

■ **1** Desk-top publishing is widely used in the production of newsletters, where type and pictures can be united within a structured, pre-set grid. The text and photographic elements are fed into the computer and projected onto the screen to enable the designer to manoeuvre them into the most effective positions.

2 Laser printers can make print-outs immediately available, as they scan the information and deliver it as hard copy. This black-and-white representation shows the positional guide of all the information that is to appear in the printed newsletter, although the photographs are represented merely as black shapes in the page. All the other elements are more or less visible in their final form.

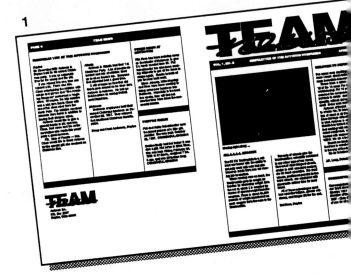

3 The front cover of this newsletter shows the degree of quality that can be achieved using the computer in the design and production process. Colours can be included, and half-tone tints and specifications can be achieved in the same way as with manual artwork production.

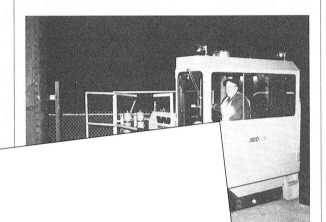

TEAM *news*

VOL. 1, NO. 2   **NEWSLETTER OF THE AUTOCON COMPANIES**   **APRIL 1988**

WELCOME TO DETROIT

I've never seen anything like it. The more I learn about Autocon, the more incredible it becomes.

I have been a union steward for 12 of the 14 years I've been in warehousing. For 14 years, I have watched the companies try desperately to obtain quality and quantity, without damage, but to no avail! Many went broke trying.

Autocon of Detroit never ceases to amaze me. To have exact location of stock at all times, and to have damage virtually disappear, is what Autocon is all about. Morale has turned around 180°. I feel working with clean, sophisticated equipment, and being treated with respect, has alot to do with it. We are a team.

There's no doubt about it. When it comes to warehousing, Autocon is the way of the future.

Go for it Autocon of Detroit!

J.R. Long, Detroit

CONGRATULATIONS

Our congratulations also go out to our Team Member of the Third Quarter, 1987 - Don Lee and Team Member of the Fourth Quarter, 1987 - Chris Rihm, both from Metrocon .Thanks for all your hard work.

...wheels give the ...ersatility not found ...e of car mover. ...flanged wheels, ...andard contour, ...ation. The road ...d parallel to the ...equipped with ...tires for road

...antages spell ...e, greater effi- ...life for the unit.

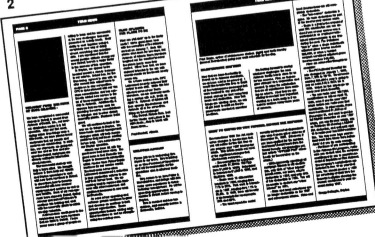

2

Grids and styling

GRIDS AND THEIR COMPLEXITIES support the thought processes behind a design concept. They are the point from which a piece of design work takes off. They are created not to confuse or to make a job more difficult but to unravel the complexities that lie beneath the design concept. They are compositional vehicles for solving design problems.

Some designers, after many years of creative exploration, devise grid formulae that appear so complex it is difficult for the untrained eye to fathom how the grid can be used. The difference between these grids and the more common format grids may be compared to the difference between an architect's blueprints for, say, a massive shopping centre and those for a simple home.

Once the grid has been established, it becomes a tool for the evolution of a design. In its most developed form, this evolution is the most creative activity of all, an activity in which the design elements may develop beyond the grid itself.

On the other hand, the grid can be used to solve a design problem. This tends to happen more when many of the components remain constant throughout the design concept. The grids can be used and worked on by different designers simultaneously, and yet the overall design will retain a visual consistency.

In this book I have shown how simple, functional grids can be developed and how these act as a framework for your design. We have looked at the underlying construction of some popular pieces of print and have observed a designer as he carries out the processes of design within a given context. In addition, we have seen how a grid is formulated. From all this I hope you will find grids an easier and more readily accessible basis for your own work.

1

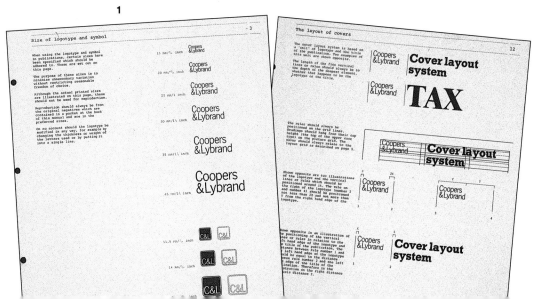

■ 1 Corporate design manuals are set out by the designer to give subsequent designers specific style guidelines in the positioning and structuring of a company's image. Systems, proportions, sizes are all included in this manual to ensure that future designs are formulated through a structured, grid-based system.

2

3

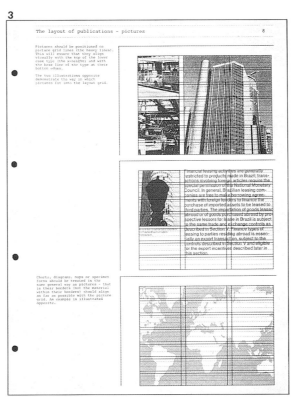

2 & 3 Page layouts, page divisions, type size and picture framing are all governed by the manual's grid instructions. The correct proportions and type size can easily be located in this information.

4 & 5 Even the positioning of the same graphic elements is pre-determined, giving a number of alternative design solutions for the designer to follow. The paper proportions and sizes that are acceptable to the company are specified and illustrated.

4

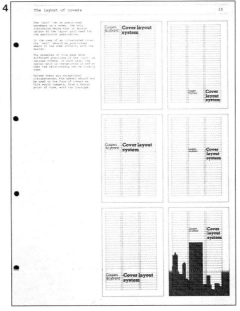

5

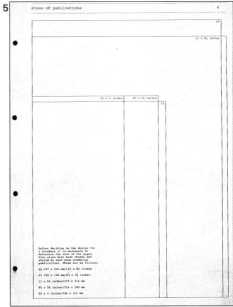

Glossary

Artwork Any type of image that is of a high enough standard to be reproduced.

Ascenders The stroke that, in lower case letters, rises above the main part of the letter.

Bembo The name used for a particular typeface; the body text of this book is set in Bembo.

Binding The term most often used when printed pages are secured in an outer cover.

Bleed The term used to describe that area of an image designed to extend to the edges of the trimmed sheet without any free space or margins.

Body copy The main part of the written matter as opposed to the headings and so on.

Bromide Paper with a photosensitive coating that is used when an image has to be reproduced photographically.

Capitals The large, upper case letters of a typeface, as opposed to the lower case letters.

Characters The word used in typography to describe letters, punctuation marks and space between words.

Column An arrangement of text on lines, one above the other, with each line of roughly equal length.

Compositor The person who, in the printing process, composes type in the typesetting machine. Nowadays this is normally fed into a computer.

Cropping Ls L-shaped, interlocking pieces of paper or card used by designers to place over photographs or transparencies to help in the decision-making process. The Ls act as a framing device so that the designer can decide how to trim the illustrative matter.

Depth gauge (or scale) A rule for measuring lines of type at different point sizes.

Descenders The stroke that, in lower case letters, sinks below the main part of the letter.

Em The square of the body of any size of type. The 12pt em, or pica, is used for the linear measurement of type. Half the width of an Em is known as an En.

Four-colour process The process of reproducing full colour by separating the image into three primary colours – cyan, magenta and yellow – plus black. Each of the four colours is carried on a separate plate, which, when printed over each other, reproduces the effect of all the colours in the original.

Galleys The columns of text that are produced uncut from the typesetting machinery. These are used both for proof checking and making up layouts.

Grids The sheets used in design to represent a spread or design area on which all the relevant measurements – page size, margins, trim marks and so on – are printed. This enables the designer accurately to place all the components.

Gutter The inner margin between the printed area and the binding on a page of a book or magazine.

Illustration The term used to describe an image that has been drawn as opposed to one that has been photographed.

Image The visual subject matter of an illustration, design or photograph.

Justified The term used to describe lines of text that are spaced and set to align with both the left- and right-hand margins.

Key lines The outlines of an artwork, which act as a guide to the printer for the positioning of colours or specific components on a layout.

Leading The space, measured in points, between lines of setting.

Logo Initials or words cast as a single unit usually as a company signature or trademark.

Lower case The small letters of a typeface, as opposed to the capitals.

Margin The blank areas at the edges of a page that surround all the printed matter.

Masthead The title and/or logo of a magazine or newspaper as it appears on the front cover.

Packaging A pack or carton that is constructed of card and designed for an individual product.

Photomechanical transfer (PMT) A process accomplished with a camera with a variety of functions, including changing black to white and vice versa, converting colour to black and white, scaling up and down and producing screened halftones. The quality achieved is high enough for reproduction.

Photosetting A form of typesetting that is photographically produced on to film or bromide. The quality is good enough for direct reproduction and it is extremely versatile.

Pica-em The term used to denote the measure often used to determine the width of columns of setting.

Point A measure used to describe the size of typography and spacing. A point is 0.351mm, and the system is used mainly in the UK and America; the Didot point is favoured in other parts of the world. The two systems are not interchangeable.

Presentation visual Any graphic material or illustrations executed for the purpose of showing the client what the proposed design or finished product will look like.

Printer's proof The initial sheets printed prior to the actual print run on which the printer and designer make any final adjustments to the colour or tone.

Range Text is said to be ranged when it is set to align either with the left- or right-hand margin.

Registration marks The marks that are carried on artworks, overlays, films and so on to ensure that the image can be accurately positioned and that each piece of film aligns precisely with the others when superimposed during reproduction.

Reverse out The term used to describe the process by which an image appears white out of a solid background. It is usually achieved by photomechanical transfer techniques.

Sans serif The term used to describe typefaces that do not have small terminal strokes on the individual letters.

Scholar's margin A wide margin at the outer edge of the page on which the reader may make notes about the text.

Serifs The small terminating strokes on individual letters.

Sub-heading A heading used to break up a chapter or page in a publication.

Text The main body of words in any publication.

Thumbnail sketch A very rough, small and quick initial sketch that is used to work out an idea.

Tint A faint colour often used as a background before printing.

Tone The varying shades of a single colour.

Tracing paper A translucent paper that can be placed over an image so that the image can still be seen clearly, thus enabling the outline to be followed in pencil or pen.

Trim marks Marks made on a sheet to indicate where the printed pages can be cut and trimmed.

Type rule A ruler on which the divisions are calculated using the point system. It is used for measuring column widths and type specifications.

Typeface A general term used to describe all the various styles of lettering available in typesetting.

Typesetting The assembly of type for printing by hand, machine or photographic techniques.

Typography The art, general design and appearance of printed matter using type.

X-height The height of lower case letters without ascenders or descenders.

Index

Acknowledgements

Every effort has been made to obtain copyright clearance for the illustrations used in this book and we do apologize if any omissions have been made. Quarto would like to thank the following for their help with this publication:

p10–11 *left to right* Collett Dickenson Pearce, Dennard Creative, Texas, the *Guardian, Elle,* Trickett & Webb, *Parents.* **p28** John Scorey. **p45** Valerie Bennett/Architectural Association. **p57** David Quay, London; reproduced with permission of the Monotype Corporation plc. **p58** Malcom Carrett, Assorted Images. **p59** Lone Case Associates, Toronto. **p60–63** David Quay, London; reproduced with permission of the Monotype Corporation plc. **p65** Collett Dickenson Pearce. **p66–67** Boase Massimi Pollitt. **p68–69** The Small Back Room. **p70–71** Samenwerkende Ontwerpers, Amsterdam. **p72–73** Robin Johnson Design, London; designer, Barry Killick; illustrator, Victor Ambros; printer, Westerham Press; client, The Ministry of Defence. **p74–75** Trickett & Webb Ltd. **p76** David Quay, reproduced by kind permission of Esselte Electraset Ltd. **p77** *left* David Quay, reproduced by kind permissin of Esselte Electraset Ltd; *right* Edward Briscoe Assoc. **p78–79** Trickett & Webb Ltd. **p80–81** the *Guardian.* **p82** Caroline Grimshaw, EMAP Metro. **p83** Graham Ogilvie, *Parents.* **p84–85** *Elle.* **p86** Trickett & Webb Ltd. **p87** *top* Quarto Publishing; *bottom* Trickett & Webb Ltd. **p88–89** Quarto Publishing. **p90–91** The Design Solution; Client John Faith and Co. **p95-101, 105–115** *Elle.* **p136–137** Greg Cutshaw, Ohio. **p138–139** Cooper & Lybrand. **p134–135** Quarto Publishing.